"In this highly readable, down-to-earth, and practical self-help book, Elliot Cohen skillfully guides the reader through the process of ridding the emotional, behavioral, and interpersonal ravages of perfectionism. Not a one-step-fits-all approach, this book lays out ten discreet varieties of perfectionism for an individual to self-diagnose, and shows how to use a straightforward, six-step method to bring both relief and peace of mind. As a practicing rational emotive behavior therapist, I will make sure to keep copies available for all my patients."

—**Russell Grieger, PhD**, clinical psychologist in private practice, organizational consultant, and adjunct professor at the University of Virginia; author of *The Couples Therapy Companion*, *Developing Unrelenting Drive, Dedication, and Determination*, and the forthcoming *The Serious Business of Being Happy*

"Elliot Cohen continues to prove to be the heir to Albert Ellis. In this accessible and instructive new book, Cohen provides hope to those struggling with perfectionism. In extending his logic-based therapeutic approach to combating various forms of obsessionality and self-defeating thoughts and attitudes, he provides a practical six-step method to overcome perfectionistic tendencies and embrace the courage to be imperfect. A classic self-help guidebook."

—**Jon Mills, PsyD, PhD, ABPP**, professor in the department of psychology and psychoanalysis at the Adler Graduate Professional School in Toronto, ON, Canada; and author of *Inventing God*

"An excellent, exhaustive analysis of perfectionism from the perspective of Albert Ellis's rational emotive behavior therapy (REBT). Clearly, interestingly, and incisively written, it takes the reader through a guided tour of the various types of perfectionism, the many circumstances under which they occur, their pernicious consequences, and effective strategies for combating them. I highly recommend this book for anyone whose life is diminished by a perfectionistic outlook. You may be surprised by the depth and comprehensiveness of its presence in your own daily functioning."

> —**Michael R. Edelstein, PhD**, clinical psychologist, former training supervisor and fellow of the Albert Ellis Institute, and author of *Three Minute Therapy*

"Most books on cognitive behavioral therapy (CBT) are written by psychologists; this one is written by a philosopher with a fine grasp of CBT and psychological issues. Standing on the shoulders of philosophical giants, Cohen takes a compassionate view of the human condition and our tendency to ask too much from ourselves and others. He engages us in the wisdom of history's finest thinkers and greatest achievers, inviting us to choose the paths that lead from our personal perfectionism to greater freedom and enjoyment of an imperfect but worthwhile life."

> —**Irwin F. Altrows, PhD**, psychologist in private practice, and adjunct assistant professor in the department of psychology and psychiatry at Queen's University in Kingston, ON, Canada

"'Nobody's perfect, Dad,' my then-eight-year-old daughter reminded me decades ago. Alas, many of us make 'perfect' the standard for our own behavior, when 'excellent,' 'fine,' or even 'good' would carry the day. We're human. Everyone makes mistakes.

Making Peace with Imperfection clearly and systematically addresses the destructive beliefs and behavior patterns that cause perfectionism, offering a six-step procedure for dealing with each of the ten types of perfectionism, integrating philosophical insights with empirically validated interventions from rational emotive behavior therapy, and helping readers devise a personalized approach. This book belongs in the personal growth toolbox of everyone for whom perfect is the enemy of good."

—**Robert E. Alberti, PhD**, retired psychologist, professor, author, editor, publisher, and coauthor of *Your Perfect Right*

"A remarkable book, full of helpful techniques for combating the core schema that produce most of the self-inflicted emotional disturbances: perfectionist demands placed on oneself, others, and the world. Especially helpful is the breaking down of perfectionism into the categories of absolutistic needs for achievement, approval, control, and certainty; and how they inevitably produce most emotional disturbances and dysfunctional behavior. The book provides exceptionally helpful rational countermessages for helping people get unstuck from their low self-esteem, depression, anger, anxiety, and low frustration tolerance, as well as techniques to help them better deal with the dysfunctional behaviors that accompany them. Albert Ellis would consider this book as close to perfect as possible in implementing his theory and practice."

—**Janet Wolfe, PhD**, former director of the Albert Ellis Institute

Making Peace with
IMPERFECTION

Discover Your Perfectionism Type,

End the Cycle of Criticism,

and Embrace Self-Acceptance

ELLIOT D. COHEN, PhD

Impact Publishers, Inc.

Publisher's Note

This publication is designed to provide accurate and authoritative information in regard to the subject matter covered. It is sold with the understanding that the publisher is not engaged in rendering psychological, financial, legal, or other professional services. If expert assistance or counseling is needed, the services of a competent professional should be sought.

Book printed in the United States of America

Distributed in Canada by Raincoast Books

Copyright © 2019 by Elliot D. Cohen
                  Impact Publishers
                  An imprint of New Harbinger Publications, Inc.
                  5674 Shattuck Avenue
                  Oakland, CA 94609
                  www.newharbinger.com

Cover design by Amy Daniel

Acquired by Jess O'Brien

Edited by Kristi Hein

All Rights Reserved

Library of Congress Cataloging-in-Publication Data on file

21   20   19

10   9   8   7   6   5   4   3   2   1   First Printing

To the late Albert Ellis, whose rational therapy
saved millions from the perils of perfectionism.

Contents

Foreword

Perfectionism is the bane of many who feel pressured, stressed, and miserable because they wrongly make their human value depend on their work performances, how well they get along with others, controlling uncertain conditions, and more. Perpetual stress also is on the horizon for those who expect others to think and behave in a certain way, and for life to unfold blissfully.

Unlike standards for excellence, perfectionism standards for attaining self-worth are preludes for feeling like a failure even if you achieve eminent successes. Worse, striving for something that cannot be detracts from having quality relationships and an enjoyable career. Lessen this toxic form of perfectionism and you can lessen these related problems as well.

There is more. When perfectionism cuts across different forms of depression, anxiety, and other unpleasant states, perfectionism balloons the misery. Decreasing toxic forms of perfectionism can lessen these conditions simultaneously (Lowndes et al., 2018).

As with his exceptional books on other topics, in *Making Peace with Imperfectionism* Dr. Elliot D. Cohen skillfully explains a six-step method to neutralize destructive perfectionism beliefs. He walks you through each step, using different forms of perfectionism as examples. He describes how you can practice combating perfectionism effectively. This preparation can benefit you in spontaneously arising situations where you might otherwise automatically step into a perfectionism trap.

Dr. Cohen outlines behavioral assignments that you can carry out on your own. Engage in these experiments, and you roll the dice in favor of quicker and more durable freedom from the afflictions of perfectionism. This is not busywork. There is a science behind this classic self-help reading approach. Indeed, active participation in this bibliotherapy process is one of the most productive things you can do to help yourself; perhaps it is the most productive (see Kazantzis et al., 2018).

Actively experiment with Dr. Cohen's six-step method, and by the time you finish this book, you will have rational reasons to believe you won't be perfect and that you don't have to be. But that doesn't mean you'll slack off, as many believe they'll do if they don't drive themselves. Instead, you may discover a paradox. When you focus your attention on what you can do, without the mental clutter of destructive perfectionism thinking, you are likely to do better with less stress. With fewer toxic perfectionistic ideas dominating your perspective on life, you'll probably have better relationships and enjoy your life more. Of course, there can be no guarantees of this, just good probabilities.

A main part of psychologist Dr. Albert Ellis's rational emotive behavior therapy is that of combating harmful irrational beliefs. Ellis's approach is amply supported by scientific research (David et al., 2018). In this book, Dr. Cohen takes a rational emotive behavioral approach to combat perfectionism. He sees the perils of perfectionist beliefs, actively shows readers how to undermine this thinking, and does a magnificent job of applying and expanding on Ellis's clear-thinking philosophical methods to solve the problem of combating perfectionism.

Dr. Cohen uses various philosophical approaches to defuse toxic perfectionistic beliefs. One is a flip technique. For example, perfectionism is a conditional-worth idea. People who think this way are in a dichotomous thinking trap wherein they are either worthy or not, and perfection is the solution for being worthy. Here is the flip side. Both Cohen and Ellis show how to think pluralistically and to unconditionally accept yourself, to unconditionally accept others, and to unconditionally accept life.

Do you have to be perfectly acceptant? Not really. Here, acceptance means taking things as they are and not as you believe they should be. That means that if you are not acceptant 100 percent of the time, that is as it is. The aphorism "Change what you can, accept what you can't, and know the difference" captures the essence of the meaning of acceptance and your potential for applying the concept healthfully and effectively.

I strongly believe that if Albert Ellis were alive today, he'd happily write the foreword to this book, endorse the content, and have glowing things to say about Dr. Cohen's extraordinary effort on behalf of helping people who torment themselves with perfectionism.

If you count yourself among the millions whose expectations are too high and who have corresponding oppressive tensions, check this book out. Test a sample of exercises. I believe you'll learn much to free yourself from the perils of perfectionism and put what you learn to good use to advance your enlightened interests and to help those close to you do the same.

—Dr. Bill Knaus, EdD

Former Director, Post-Doctoral Training, Albert Ellis Institute

Author, *The Cognitive Behavioral Workbook for Anxiety* and other quality New Harbinger books

The Perils of Perfectionism, and How This Book Can Help!

This book is a compassionate handbook for people who already suspect that there is something bogus and self-defeating about their demand for perfection. If this is you, there's a good chance you have come to the right place. This book can help you to see how your perfectionism is wrecking your own life and affecting the lives of others with whom you live, work, or socialize, and what you can do about it. I offer no magic potion to solve all your headaches. That is another perfectionistic ploy.

The Difference Between Striving for Excellence and Perfectionism

Striving for excellence in things that matter to you is *not* perfectionism; indeed, it can be a healthy and productive way to live. Maybe you aspire to be the best athlete, student, cook, spouse, or attorney you can be. You are highly motivated and shoot for the stars. So far, so good! What separates such healthy aspirations from perfectionism is that you do not *demand* that you reach the stars. Further, undemanding individuals who enthusiastically strive for excellence may see the journey itself to be the most gratifying and exciting aspect of the pursuit, not whether they actually achieve some idealistic or unlikely goal. So let's be clear: I encourage you to take up the banner of striving for excellence—as long as you don't *demand* perfection.

Perfectionism Is Painful to Experience

Whether you demand perfection of yourself, others, or the world, you are setting yourself up for a life of painful, unrelenting stress. Why? Because you live in a vicious cycle of unremitting anxiety about whether your unrealistic demands on yourself, others, or the world will come to pass. And when reality falls short of your demands, as it invariably will, you needlessly experience depression, guilt, anger, or other painful emotions.

Perfectionism Causes Harm to You and to Others

This ongoing cycle of stress actually defeats your own purposes! Why? Because you, others, and the rest of the world this side of heaven are, by their nature, imperfect. As you will see in Chapter One, the stress you create by demanding perfection makes it harder for you to achieve your goals, help others do better, or improve the world situation. When you spend your life *insisting* on what is impossible or almost impossible to obtain, ironically, you are likely to accomplish less, create more problems for you and others, and do less to make the world a better place.

Rational-Emotive Behavior Therapy (REBT) Can Help

So what can you do to feel and do better? The approach taken in this book is based on a popular brand of psychotherapy known as *rational-emotive behavior therapy* (REBT), developed by the late great Albert Ellis, the grandfather of cognitive-behavioral therapy (CBT). This approach emphasizes working hard on changing thinking that leads you to act in self-defeating ways, and it helps to promote constructive cognitive change through changing the behaviors you engage in that reinforce your self-defeating thinking.

It's Not the Events in Your Life That Upset You

A key aspect of REBT is gleaned from the ancient Roman philosopher Epictetus, who astutely perceived that it's not the events in your life that upset you, but your interpretation of those events. The devil often lies in the language people use to create irrational, self-defeating interpretations of reality. "It's awful, horrible, and terrible that I lost my job. I am nothing but a worthless failure who will never amount to anything!" Such an interpretation of reality is bound to send you into an emotional tailspin, because you have used strong emotive language ("awful," "horrible," "terrible," "worthless," and "failure") to *irrationally rate or evaluate* the situation. Compare that with: "I lost my job. Tough break, but it's still not the end of the world." The language you use to interpret the same bit of reality can make an incredible difference between emotional resilience and deep dark depression.

As such, according to REBT, people cause their own behavioral and emotional problems through irrational interpretations or beliefs about life events. Chief among them is demanding perfection. "Because I *must* never lose a job, I'm now a worthless failure. How awful, horrible, and terrible!" See how that "must" can generate the rest of your self-destructive thinking?

Bad Logic Can Be Wrecking Your Personal and Interpersonal Happiness

The version of REBT applied in this book is a philosophical, logic-based one that I developed starting in the mid-1980s in collaboration with Albert Ellis. According to the logic-based version, known as *logic-based therapy*, people create their own behavioral and emotional headaches by engaging in *bad logic*. And demanding perfection is bad logic: a logical *fallacy* or mistake in reasoning. What makes demanding perfection a fallacy is that, like other fallacies, it has an established track record of frustrating the quest for personal and interpersonal happiness (Cohen, 1995). And, like other mistakes in reasoning, it involves a *faulty inference*. This means coming to a conclusion that simply doesn't follow from the premise. For example, "I *want* to keep my job, *therefore* I *must* keep it." Just because you *want* something doesn't mean it *must* be! Once you become aware of the faulty thinking behind the types of demanding perfection that frustrates your happiness, you can better see how to avoid its self-defeating inferences.

Ten Types of Perfectionism

Yes, there are different types of perfectionism, and this book addresses ten of them:

1. Achievement perfectionism

2. Approval perfectionism

3. Moral perfectionism

4. Control perfectionism

5. Expectation perfectionism

6. Ego-centered perfectionism

7. Treatment perfectionism

8. Existential perfectionism

9. Neatness perfectionism

10. Certainty perfectionism

In Chapter Two, you can take the Demanding Perfection Self-Check Inventory, which can help you identify your type/s of demanding perfection. Later you'll find straightforward methods for overcoming each type, along with systematic sets of practice exercises.

The Six-Step Method

Each step is followed by an example of how this approach works (Cohen, 2017).

Step 1: Identify your irrational thinking generated by your demand for perfection.

Example:

1. I must never fail.

2. *Therefore*, if I failed to keep my job, I'm a failure.

3. I failed to keep my job.

4. *Therefore*, I'm a failure!

Step 2: Refute the irrational premises in your thinking; that is, demonstrate that they are self-defeating, false, inconsistent, or otherwise irrational.

Example: "Inferring that I'm a failure because I failed to keep my job is like inferring that I'm a fart because I farted!"

Step 3: Identify new, rational goals—what I call "guiding virtues"—that can help you overcome your irrational premises and attain greater security in this imperfect world ("metaphysical security") (Cohen, 2017).

Example: Unconditionally accept yourself!

Step 4: Gain philosophical wisdom from the sages (great thinkers throughout history) on how to reach for your guiding virtues.

Example: Acclaimed thinker Immanuel Kant says, "Don't treat yourself like an object!"

Step 5: Build a rational plan of action that applies this wisdom.

Example: "I will stop degrading myself as if I were a defective object, and will exercise my rational self-determination to make constructive changes in my life."

Step 6: Put your plan into practice.

Example: "I'm making excellent progress, reminding myself regularly that I'm a worthy person, capable of rationally determining my life. So I start training next week in an exciting new field I've always wanted to pursue!"

Moving from Intellect to Emotional Appreciation

Overcoming your demand for perfection starts with appreciating intellectually that it is irrational, and proceeds with an evolving emotional appreciation. Steps 1 through 4 can help you gain an *intellectual* appreciation of just how irrational and self-destructive your demand really is, and how you can reframe your thinking.

- **Step 1** shows you what your perfectionistic thinking looks like.

- **Step 2** shows you exactly what's wrong with this thinking.

- **Step 3** replaces your self-defeating demand for perfection with new, rational goals for living contentedly in an imperfect world.

- **Step 4** gives you the wisdom of the sages to work toward these new goals.

Steps 5 and 6 offer the key to an *emotional* appreciation of the irrational, unrealistic, and self-defeating nature of demanding perfection in an imperfect world:

- **Step 5** applies the wisdom gleaned in step 4 to build an action plan to better manage the challenges of living in an imperfect world.

- **Step 6** puts your plan into practice.

The more you engage your new philosophic wisdom in practice, the more likely you are to feel more comfortable, freer, and less encumbered by self-imposed demands. This movement from intellectual to emotional appreciation will be gradual and will continually evolve.

Maybe you're saying, "Yes, I see it is irrational to demand perfection of myself in a world that is inherently flawed, and to degrade myself when I fall short. But I still *feel* down when I make a mistake or don't do a perfect or near-perfect job. I can tell myself that I'm still a worthy person, but I just don't feel like one."

Don't despair! In this state of cognitive dissonance, where the conflict between your reason and your emotion has risen to the level of conscious awareness, lies the possibility of constructive change. For change is possible only when you first recognize what needs to change (Cohen, 2007). The rest is about gradually increasing your *willpower* to overcome your old self-defeating, painful ways of thinking and acting by replacing them with more constructive ones. The prime goal is therefore to bring emotion in line with reason, which means feeling comfortable with the world as it is, not as it *must* be.

You Can Develop Metaphysical Security

The use of strong, emotive language—especially the four-letter word "must"—to *demand* perfection about the world belies a fundamental *mis*-interpretation of the world. From antiquity, philosophers have pondered the question of what is real—the central problem of the field of philosophy known as metaphysics. Invariably, these philosophers have dismissed the idea that the world we inhabit is perfect. From ancient thinkers like Buddha, who held that demanding permanence in an ever-changing world leads to needless suffering, to contemporary thinkers like Bertrand Russell, who admonished us not to demand certainty, great minds have consistently instructed us that if we are to live happily we must accept the imperfect nature of our world. As such, these sages have pointed to the most basic human virtue: accepting and feeling comfortable with reality, notwithstanding its imperfections. I call this crowning virtue *metaphysical security* (Cohen, 2007), and it is a prime goal of this book to help you on your way toward attaining it.

Drawing on Historical Thinkers to Become More Metaphysically Secure

You will be in excellent company on your journey to becoming more metaphysically secure! The history of thought contains gems of wisdom that can help you create a rational plan of action to overcome your self-defeating emotions and behavior that stem from demanding perfection and to attain greater metaphysical security. For example, ancient Stoic philosophers such as Epictetus admonish us to distinguish between the things within our control and those outside of it; modern thinkers like the contemporary French existentialist Jean-Paul Sartre instruct us to accept probability, not certainty, as part of the human condition. So if you demand that you always, or almost always, be in control, or demand certainty before you are willing to act, these profound thinkers can help you formulate philosophically enlightened ways to reframe your thinking and acting to improve your self-control, foresight, courage, prudence, and other rational habits to manage the challenges of human existence.

Metaphysical security is multidimensional because there are so many different aspects of reality. You cannot control everything in the world, be certain about the future, always have everything neat and tidy, never have anything bad happen to you, always be treated fairly by others, and so forth. As such, there are different types of metaphysical security. For example, *authenticity* is a type of security that can help you overcome self-defeating demands for approval; *unconditional self-acceptance* is a type that can help you overcome perfectionistic and self-abasing demands to achieve. Again, I call these types of metaphysical security *guiding virtues*. As virtues, they represent human excellence: habits developed and reinforced through practice, to manage excellently, but never perfectly, the challenges of living in an imperfect world. These rational goals for overcoming your perfectionistic thinking are discussed in detail in Chapter Three.

How to Read This Book

This book is concise and intended to serve your purposes as directly as possible. It's constructed so you can begin exploring the types of demanding perfection that are most problematic for you. The first three chapters offer information that applies to any type of perfectionism; the remaining chapters (except for the final one) each address a specific type and do not depend on your having read any of the other chapters. The Demanding Perfection Self-Check Inventory in Chapter Two can help you identify specific chapters to focus on. However, you may find referrals in one chapter to another to be relevant to you, and you may later want to read a chapter you didn't initially think was relevant to you.

Keep a Journal!

I'd like you to start a journal to record your responses to the book exercises. Use paper and pen or create a doc file to enter and save your responses. Writing things down is helpful because expressing your thoughts in words actually clarifies what you are thinking, and you can consult your entries later.

Doing the exercises is key to overcoming your particular type/s of perfectionism. Each exercise set requires you to push yourself to do things you may feel disinclined to do. This is the nature of a habit. It offers resistance. But there is an immeasurable reward in freeing yourself from an oppressive habit. And to reinforce the constructive changes you make, the final step for each type requires you to reward yourself when you accomplish something in your plan of action. This can be anything you really like: your favorite food, entertainment, or whatever floats your boat, as long as it's legal!

CHAPTER 1

Demanding Perfection: What It Is and Why It's Self-Destructive

Do you tell yourself that you are a perfectionist? Do you wear this title like a badge of honor even though it is wrecking your life? You may insist there's a silver lining to the pains you take to be perfect. After all, good things come with a price. Maybe up to now you have been willing to feel disturbed when you, others (especially those you love), or the world fails to be perfect. Maybe you see it as simply the cost of attaining happiness, the welfare of others, or the prosperity of the world in the long run. Maybe you tell yourself this. But where's your proof? How many years have you shaved off of your life "waiting for Godot" like the characters in Samuel Beckett's play—telling yourself there will be a payoff for your perfectionism in some added personal, spiritual, moral, social, human, or even religious value that comes sometime, somewhere, somehow? Of course, you mean well. You want the best, the absolute best—or damn near it. What's wrong with that?

What's wrong is that your *demanding* perfection, not just wanting or preferring it, is standing in the way of the good things you are seeking. It's creating needless, self-defeating stress—anxiety, anger, guilt, or even depression.

How This Demand Works

This demand has certain features that work together to produce these stressful, self-defeating results. Though you are sincere and committed to doing what is right and good, the logic of your demand can sabotage your efforts. How does demanding perfection in this self-defeating way appear in your life?

Your "Musts" Become Laws

You *mus*turbate about the thing (or things) in question—that is, you think that it *must* be, thus setting up a pseudo law of nature. For example, you think that bad things must never happen to you or to your loved ones. So, as with the law of gravity and its corollary—"Whatever goes up *must* come down"—you invent an artificial law stipulating that no serious harm comes to you or your loved ones. Indeed, such things might happen to someone else, but never to you or the ones you love!

Any Alternatives Just "Can't" Happen

You therefore *can't*stipate about it by telling yourself that it *can't* be any other way, and you refuse to entertain any other possibilities. "I just *can't* settle for anything less than an A on that test!" For you, the world offers no other acceptable options; anything else is unthinkable!

It's an All-or-Nothing Game

Your demand is therefore *absolute*, admitting no exceptions. "I must *always* have the approval of others, or at least the people who are important to me." "I must *never* fail at anything, or at least at anything at which I actually try to succeed." In doggedly applying such an all-or-nothing logic to a variable universe, you foreclose the opportunity to deal rationally with the inevitability of disappointment.

The Bar Is Set Beyond What's Possible

Your demand is also *idealistic*, which means that it is not realistic—it's either impossible to be satisfied or extremely unlikely. "I have to always be in control"; "I must never make any mistakes"; "People must always agree with me or share my views." Here you harden your preferences for control, flawlessness, agreeability, and compatibility into an unrealizable demand.

Your Demand Is Groundless

It is therefore *anti-empirical*—you do not base your *must*urbatory, *can't*stipated, absolutistic, idealistic demands on evidence. "I need to be loved by everyone." "I must always know the answers to questions that I'm asked." "Others must always meet up to my expectations." But where's the evidence to prove that you actually *need* to be loved by everyone, that you must know it all, or that others must measure up to your expectations? True, you would prefer these things, but that does not mean that you *must* have them. Unfortunately, this inference tends to go unnoticed by so many who live in a state of unrelenting stress.

So Many Demand Perfection

In fact, in one study I conducted, almost half of a sample of 2,186 mostly college students ranging in ages from late teens to sixty-four demanded perfection at least some of the time. This evidence emerges from a computer program I created that scans people's personal essays searching for faulty thinking. It asks certain questions when it finds key terms connected to particular faulty thinking errors. In the case of demanding perfection, the program looks for "musts" (or synonyms). When it finds a *must*, it asks if the term is being used to make one of these perfectionistic demands:

- I must always, or almost always, do well (in at least some things).

- I must always, or almost always, be right or do what is right.

- I must always, or almost always, get love or approval from (at least certain) others.

- I must always, or almost always, be treated well by (at least certain) others.

- Things in my life must always, or almost always, go the way I want or intend them to go.

Out of 2,176 people, 1,011 responded "Yes/Probably" to confirm that they were demanding perfection in at least one of the listed ways. That's about 47 percent, which is a lot of people demanding that the world be what it cannot be: perfect! So you are definitely not alone in making unrealistic demands on yourself, others, or the world!

The Views of Metaphysically Secure People

Fortunately, there is a healthy alternative to demanding perfection: developing the metaphysical security we have touched on. Metaphysically secure people are comfortable with these inherent, unavoidable imperfections in reality:

- You are not perfect—not even near-perfect.

- Other people are also not perfect, or even near-perfect.

- Justice and fairness do not always prevail.

- Other people will not always like or approve of you.

- Other people will not, nor are they required to, always agree with you, even on important matters.

- Other people will not always treat you fairly.

- Shit does, indeed, happen.

- The world is not necessarily neat and orderly.

- You cannot always control the bad things that happen.

- The future is inherently uncertain.

Therefore, metaphysically secure people:

- Avoid extreme thinking; for example, "Either I'm perfect or I'm worthless"; "If I don't know something, then I'm stupid"; "I am either a success or a failure."

- Are neither pie-in-the-sky optimists nor unwieldy pessimists, but instead take the middle ground of being reasonably hopeful.

- Do not spend their lives lamenting the imperfections in the world but instead see them as opportunities for constructive growth and change.

It does take some measure of *courage* to face reality as it is, and in your actions to remain mindful of its inherent risks. In this way, guiding virtues like courage, authenticity, self-control, decisiveness, tolerance, self-respect, empathy, and prudence form an interlocking network of mutually supportive dimensions of metaphysical security.

Of course, there are different types of demanding perfection, and thus different ways in which you, in particular, may be insecure about reality. We'll address these different types of demanding perfection in Chapter Two, where you will begin to explore the particular way, or ways, *you* may be demanding perfection. This book will help you work on strengthening the particular virtues that relate most directly to the specific insecurities that lead you to demand perfection.

Recovery, Not Cure!

There is a close analogy between being addicted and demanding perfection. In both cases, you have an unrelenting demand or craving. As with the temporary fix of alcohol or a narcotic, you may feel satisfied when you think something positive is at hand. But then you find a flaw, something missed, a failing, an indelible spot, or something fell short of the perfection you demanded. This insatiable and ever-present demand can, like a substance addiction, affect how you live and what you do. So, while the addict's life activities may revolve around drinking or drugging, a demander of perfection may also:

- Reject and avoid others who do not see eye to eye with them

- Refuse to take risks

- Do self-defeating things, just to get the approval of others

- Adjust their life around the perfectionistic demand

Demands for perfection can lead to personal and interpersonal problems, much like an addiction to alcohol or drugs. They can destroy intimate relationships, lead to divorce, thwart job success, or otherwise defeat the very goals that you may have set for yourself.

As with an addiction, you are also subject to relapses when you are "on the wagon" from demanding perfection. That is, in working through your perfectionism you are always subject to lapses of demanding perfection. Thus, the model proposed in this book is appropriately called a *recovery model*. As a recovering perfectaholic, you will always be in recovery. This means it's not a good idea to declare yourself "cured"—for as soon as you do, you are likely to start demanding perfection again, and make excuses for doing so.

As with an addiction, there is also a tendency to deny that there is anything wrong with demanding perfection; and like a social drinker, you may find yourself claiming that it is socially acceptable—even admirable—to be a perfectaholic. And of course you may think you can quit any time you want. Wrong! I'll explain why in the next section.

The Biology of a Bad Habit

Demanding perfection can be a way of life. It can affect virtually every decision you make and every action you take, leading to a life of perpetual stress, whereby you make unrealistic, self-defeating demands about everyday life matters, from the smallest tasks to life-altering ones. If this sounds a lot like you, then you have a bad habit! You have gotten yourself used to constantly demanding perfection in an imperfect world. Now you need to get yourself *unused* to it!

How do you get into bad habits? You repeatedly do something. So how do you get out of bad habits? You stop doing the things that support the bad habit.

Now, demanding perfection can be a very deep and pervasive habit indeed. It not only has cognitive and behavioral tentacles; it also has emotional ones. So you *feel* compelled to demand perfection. It feels right to you, and you may feel uncomfortable—very uncomfortable—about not having perfection, as though you have an intense itch that you are not scratching. This itch-scratch analogy is actually a good one, because there is a neurological basis to the discomfort of not having perfection when you are habitually disposed to demand it. Your brain and nervous system have been conditioned to demand perfection as a way of coping with stimuli from the outside world.

For example, someone acts unfriendly to you, and you immediately become apprehensive and demand that this person be accepting of you. In the language of brain science, a part of your brain called the amygdala springs into action. This is an emotive center of your brain that responds to perceived danger. If you demand approval of others, this part of your brain will go off when you perceive (correctly or incorrectly) that somebody has not approved of you. In this case, the part of your brain known as the neocortex—the thinking, practical decision-making part of your brain—lets the amygdala know that there is danger afoot, and the amygdala in turn signals other parts of your body such as the hypothalamus to prepare your body for the onslaught. So there are endocrine changes in your body (for example, increased stress hormones in your blood) and peripheral nervous system changes (your body readies to protect itself from the danger). If your neocortex has been conditioned to demand approval of others, this sets off a chain of bodily changes that creates a stressful emotional response, including uncomfortable sensations. In this case, return to normalcy or homeostasis is linked to getting rid of the stressor—namely, eliminating the lack of approval.

How Can You Overcome This Self-Defeating Habit?

The sort of practice necessary for making lasting changes involves changing the perfectionistic ways you think and respond to life situations. Since there are such deep physiological roots to the habit of demanding perfection, getting rid of the problem will require serious work. You will need to change your ordinary way of responding to *not* satisfying your perfectionistic demand. This requires that you:

- Work diligently to change your thinking and ordinary responses to *not* satisfying your demand for perfection

- Learn new ways of coping with your environment instead of demanding perfection of it

- Practice these new coping mechanisms so new brain changes (new neurological pathways) replace the old, self-defeating set of responses

After completing Chapters Two and Three, you will have an opportunity to work on making these constructive changes by applying the six-step, logic-based REBT method (as described in the introduction) to the specific ways in which you demand perfection.

It's Going to Take Willpower!

Making such changes will take willpower! Willpower is like a muscle; it gets stronger the more you exercise it. So it's going to take serious practice, but it will be worth it in the amount of stress you'll avoid and the sense of freedom you'll enjoy—freedom from the tormenting strain of demanding perfection and never seeming to achieve it.

Get to the Root of Your Emotional Stress

According to logic-based therapy, demanding perfection is the master fallacy—the fallacy from which all or most other fallacies that create behavioral and emotional headaches are inferred. If you demand perfection, you can bet your last dollar there are other fallacies inferred from it that are also helping to frustrate your personal and interpersonal happiness. For example, suppose you demand that you never make mistakes, and you just made one at work. You gave a presentation before the company bigwigs and stumbled over your words. "What a stupid idiot," you say to yourself. "How could I have gotten up there and made a total fool of myself?" Here, in using the negatively charged terms "stupid idiot" and "total fool," you degrade yourself as *totally worthless*. In so doing, you feel hopeless and demoralized, and you foresee your future prospects for happiness in the bleakest of terms.

Well, if you put on your critical thinking cap, you can see that your self-worth was not flushed down the toilet with your mistake. That's a fallacy, and it is fueled by the demand that you not make any mistakes. That's one type of demand for perfection (taken up in Chapter Four), and, as you can see, like a virus, it can lead to more serious infections. Before you know it, you are ready to throw yourself onto the junk heap! This book will help you identify such *syndromes* of fallacies (Cohen, 2003) that can be your own undoing, but only if you (that's right, *you*) let them!

Refute Your *Must*

Refuting the *must* within your demands—proving to yourself that it is irrational and self-defeating—is key to your happiness, because as long as you keep telling yourself that the world must exist in some state of ideality, you banish yourself to a life out of sync with the imperfect nature of the universe and its cosmic inventory, including human nature. So you tell yourself you *must* always succeed. But sooner or later, inevitably, you will fall short of your absolutistic goal. Unfortunately, failure is something you just *can't* accept. Consequently, you walk a tightrope without a net, carrying the angst of what to you is unthinkable: that you will eventually fail. It is not that you courageously confront the inevitability of failing, like the tightrope walker who faces the peril of walking the line without a net precisely because it is death defying. Rather, you do not even accept the dreaded possibility of failing. So today maybe you have succeeded, but there is always tomorrow, when failure is still possible, or the next day, or the next, and so on. Your only escape from this kaleidoscope of stress is to come clean and give up your *must*; to give yourself permission to be human—which means accepting that you are imperfect. Ah, freedom! It feels so good when you let go of that damn *must*!

Think about it. If you *must* be perfect, then you *would* be perfect because *must* implies necessity, which means it could not be any other way. But you are *not* perfect. Nobody is. Have you ever been jealous, gotten angry unnecessarily, believed falsely, misjudged something or someone, drew an illogical inference, forgotten something, or treated someone unfairly? If you are honest (and human), you will answer a resounding *yes*! And I suspect you can add many other things to the list to prove the point that you are not even near-perfect. This is nothing personal. It's just the way human beings (including yours truly) are:

imperfect. Therefore, your demand that you *must* be perfect or near-perfect is hereby refuted. It is contradicted by human nature itself. In other words, *there is a contradiction in demanding that an imperfect being be perfect, or that a less-than-near-perfect being be near-perfect.*

And here's the crux of the matter: your inference from what you want or prefer to what *must* be is self-disturbing and irrational. No doubt you prefer that the world align with your preferences. Maybe you would prefer it if you or your loved ones never got sick; if you were the wisest person on earth, never lost a loved one, and were loved by all. There's nothing wrong with wanting or preferring any of these things. But the problem starts when you conclude that therefore it *must* be so. Metaphysically secure people avoid such inferences because they are at home in a world in which they don't necessarily get what they want or prefer. In fact, such people prefer that they not get everything they prefer. As the philosopher and psychologist William James astutely observed, a world in which we necessarily got what we preferred would be a boring world. It would leave little to which to aspire, since our dreams and wishes would automatically be fulfilled. It would be a world without risk because we would automatically succeed. Such a "perfect" world would be a sanitized universe in which freedom could only mean "freedom to do *worse*, and who could be so insane as to wish for that?" To the contrary, James admonishes: "The only possibility that one can rationally claim is the possibility that things be *better*" (James, 1955, 85). Following James's lead, the next chapter on the journey of recovery will discuss how you can make life-changing strides toward this more exciting, fulfilling, and realistic goal of doing and feeling better in a less-than-perfect world.

CHAPTER 2

What Type of Perfectionist Are You, Anyway?

Let's get started, shall we? As mentioned in Chapter One, there are different types of demanding perfection. So, while you may demand perfection in some ways, you may not do so in other ways. This means that some chapters, which address specific types of demanding perfection, may be more or less relevant to you, depending on the way (or ways) in which you demand perfection. You should be open to the possibility of more than one type of perfectionism relevant to your case.

The set of ten self-check statements in the Demanding Perfection Self-Check Inventory in Exercise 2.1 can help you identify the ways in which you may be demanding perfection. Each describes emotional experiences associated with a specific type of perfectionism, as confirmed by a growing body of research on perfectionism (Cohen, 2012; Flett, Greene, & Hewitt, 2004; Hewitt & Flett, 1993). In taking the inventory, you can reflect on how you may feel in certain situations to see whether and the extent to which any of these statements apply to you.

EXERCISE 2.1. The Demanding Perfection Self-Check Inventory

For each self-check statement, indicate the frequency with which the statement applies to you. Your responses can help you determine what type or types of demanding perfection you may need to work on in subsequent chapters. Enter your responses in your journal.

1. I am hard on myself when I fail, make a mistake, or otherwise fall short of my goal. In such cases, I experience self-doubts, put myself down, or keep thinking about my perceived inadequacy.

   ☐ Almost always ☐ Often ☐ Sometimes ☐ Rarely, if ever

2. I feel insecure about myself if I don't get the approval of others (or certain others), and I try very hard to get their approval.

   ☐ Almost always ☐ Often ☐ Sometimes ☐ Rarely, if ever

3. I experience strong guilt when I think I have done something morally wrong or unethical. In such cases, I question my self-worth and keep thinking about it.

   ☐ Almost always ☐ Often ☐ Sometimes ☐ Rarely, if ever

4. I experience strong anxiety about not being able to control or prevent bad things from happening to others or myself. I keep thinking about such possibilities and what I might do to prevent them.

   ☐ Almost always ☐ Often ☐ Sometimes ☐ Rarely, if ever

5. I get upset when I think that others (or certain others) have messed up or otherwise have not lived up to my expectation/s. I then take a negative attitude toward them.

   ☐ Almost always ☐ Often ☐ Sometimes ☐ Rarely, if ever

6. I get disturbed when others disagree with me, don't share my point of view, or don't want to do things my way.

   ☐ Almost always ☐ Often ☐ Sometimes ☐ Rarely, if ever

7. I get very upset when I think others have treated me badly. In such cases, I have a hard time letting it go and dealing with it in a way that does not negatively affect me behaviorally and emotionally.

   ☐ Almost always ☐ Often ☐ Sometimes ☐ Rarely, if ever

8. I get upset when I think about the bad things in my life, in the lives of others, or in the world. I keep thinking about them and have a hard time getting them out of my head and relaxing.

   ☐ Almost always ☐ Often ☐ Sometimes ☐ Rarely, if ever

9. I get upset when things are messy, out of order, or not in the condition I think they must be.

   ☐ Almost always ☐ Often ☐ Sometimes ☐ Rarely, if ever

10. I experience anxiety when there is a possibility, even a very small one, of something bad happening, or having happened, and it makes it difficult for me to relax. While the assurances of others may help to some extent, the mere possibility still feels like a dark cloud hanging over me.

    ☐ Almost always ☐ Often ☐ Sometimes ☐ Rarely, if ever

If you have picked up this book for your own self-help purposes, it's likely you have checked "Almost always" or "Often" for one or more of these statements, and thus may have a strong tendency to demand perfection in that particular way. If you have indicated "Sometimes," you may still tend to demand perfection in particular situations. For example, some people demand that they never fail at certain things (such as a certain professional activity), but do not mind if they fail at other things. Further, you may not yet be sufficiently aware of the extent of your tendency to demand perfection in the given way. So I recommend taking seriously any frequency greater than "Rarely, if ever." Also, as you will see, there can be, and often are, connections between the various types of perfectionism treated in this book, so a tendency to demand perfection in some ways may lead you to demand perfection in other related ways.

The Three Categories of Perfectionism

The ten types of demanding perfection may also be classified under three general categories, depending on the object of the demand:

- Self-Regarding Perfectionism: Demanding perfection *of yourself*

- Other-Regarding Perfectionism: Demanding perfection *of others*

- World-Regarding Perfectionism: Demanding perfection *of the world*

Table 2.1 lists each type of perfectionism together with its respective category. The number for each type of perfectionism corresponds to the number for the associated statement in the self-check inventory.

TABLE 2.1. Categories of the Self-Check Inventory Perfectionism Types

Perfectionism Type	Perfectionism Category
1. Achievement	Self-Regarding
2. Approval	Self-Regarding
3. Moral	Self-Regarding
4. Control	Self-Regarding
5. Expectation	Other-Regarding
6. Ego-Centered	Other-Regarding
7. Treatment	Other-Regarding
8. Existential	World-Regarding
9. Neatness	World-Regarding
10. Certainty	World-Regarding

Now you have a name and category for each of the ways you may demand perfection. For example, if you checked "Almost always" or "Often" for statement 1 of the self-check inventory, then you appear to have a strong tendency toward achievement perfectionism. If you checked "Sometimes" for statement 10, you appear to have *some* tendency toward certainty perfectionism.

Snapshots of the Perfectionism Types

Before we get into the details in subsequent chapters, here are some concise descriptions of the ten types of perfectionism. This bird's-eye view is especially helpful for those types showing up in your responses to the self-check inventory. Again, if you selected a frequency of at least "Sometimes" for any type in the self-check inventory, then you have at least some tendency toward it.

Self-Regarding Perfectionism

- *Achievement Perfectionism.* This type involves demanding perfect or near-perfect performance at least in things that are important to you. You judge your self-worth according to this perfectionistic standard, measuring your worth as a person in terms of your achievements, or lack thereof.

- *Approval Perfectionism.* This type involves demanding that you gain the affections or approval of at least certain others. Approval perfectionists judge their self-worth based on whether or not they obtain such approval.

- *Moral Perfectionism.* This type involves demanding that you not do anything that violates your moral principles. Moral perfectionists damn themselves for their perceived transgressions.

- *Control Perfectionism.* This type involves demanding that you always or almost always control things, especially the actions and circumstances of others, to prevent bad things from happening to them. This leaves you in a perpetual state of anxiety about how to dodge the next potential problem you perceive to be on the horizon.

Other-Regarding Perfectionism

- *Expectation Perfectionism.* This type involves demanding that others, or certain others, perform perfectly or near-perfectly, not make any mistakes, and be successful at (or not fail at) at least some things deemed important by the perfectionist. Expectation perfectionists judge the worthiness of others based on whether or not they live up to such perfectionistic expectations.

- *Ego-Centered Perfectionism.* This type involves demanding that others, or certain others, share your beliefs, preferences, values, decisions, and/or interests. Ego-centered perfectionists perceive their own subjective viewpoint as the reality to which other people's subjective views must conform in order to be credible.

- *Treatment Perfectionism.* This type involves demanding that other people never or almost never treat you in ways you perceive as improper, unfair, or bad. You may consider yourself seriously harmed by such treatment even if the perceived iniquity is a relatively small one—for example, a slight or an inappropriate remark. You may find it difficult to deal rationally with the situation and move on.

World-Regarding Perfectionism

- *Existential Perfectionism.* This type involves demanding that bad things not happen in the world and that the world that *is* be as it *should* be. This could take the form of demanding that the world not include death, disease, famine, war, or starvation, but can also involve demanding that relatively minor or unfortunate things not happen, such as fender benders or not getting a job you want. It can also focus on significant others, such as problems your children may be having. When the world fails to match your ideal image of it, as will inevitably happen, you negatively perceive it in terms of its shortcomings.

- *Neatness Perfectionism.* This type involves demanding that the world be neat and tidy. It assumes that things should be arranged in a certain order, not in disarray, but in perfect condition; and that the world is not manageable or acceptable if this state is not achieved. For example, a messy house, a disorganized wardrobe, an oil stain on the driveway, or a crack in the ceiling is not acceptable and must not be tolerated.

- *Certainty Perfectionism.* This type involves demanding certainty that bad things won't happen, haven't happened, or aren't happening. Even small possibilities are inflated into serious ones, which leads to a continual state of anxiety and worry. Certainty perfectionists agonize for fear of something going wrong and that fear often leads to procrastination.

Your Perfectionistic Tendencies

You should now have a general idea of the different types of perfectionism, particularly the ones you tend toward, based on the Demanding Perfection Self-Check Inventory. By completing Exercise 2.2, you'll sum up what you've learned about yourself.

EXERCISE 2.2. Document Your Perfectionism

In your journal, create a table with three columns: the name of the perfectionism type (approval, achievement, moral, and so on), its category (self-, other-, or world-regarding), and your perceived tendency toward it (almost always, often, or sometimes). Use this to record information you gather on your tendencies to demand perfection.

CHAPTER 3

The Journey of Recovery

In Chapter One, I recommended adopting the recovery model of sub-stance addiction for the purposes of easing the grip of your demanding perfection. This means that you are always in the process of getting better and improving, but never cured. You'll need to accept that you can't ever let your guard down. If you declare yourself cured, this is the time to be most concerned, because it means that you have lapsed back into a state of demanding perfection—this time about *never* demanding perfection. "Now that I am cured, I must never demand perfection!" Oh, but it just doesn't work that way! This is instead a recipe for making yourself anxious about not demanding perfection ever again, and for feeling down when you lapse.

Better, Not Perfect

The road to recovery is therefore not one of attaining perfection, but one of getting and doing better. This book accordingly teaches thinking skills that can help you confront your problems of living with greater ease. It can help you:

- Be more comfortable with taking reasonable risks rather than demanding certainty

- Be better able to accept your own and other's limitations rather than demanding flawlessness

- Feel more secure even without the approval of others

- Handle disagreement and criticism from others with greater ease

- Feel disappointed rather than devastated when friends or relatives treat you poorly

- Deal more effectively, behaviorally and emotionally, with matters that are beyond your control

- Experience disappointment rather than despair when things go badly

- Live more comfortably in a world that lacks perfect order and tidiness

- Find it easier to accept that you, like other human beings, may not always do the right thing

- Find increasing excitement in the challenges of an imperfect universe that offers abundant opportunity for constructive change

It's these abilities that will enable you to *make peace with imperfection.* They embody the practical application of becoming more metaphysically secure. And they are what you can hope to improve on through working toward overcoming your habits of demanding perfection. *This involves replacing those self-destructive habits with habits that promote these more adaptive, constructive abilities.* Indeed, building your new positive habits can make the difference between living relatively stress-free in confronting the ups-and-downs of life, versus living with constant, needless stress. It is really exciting to experience the change! Establishing those metaphysically secure habits involves improving your ability to both intellectually and emotionally accept the imperfections of reality, which requires practice.

Meet the Guiding Virtues!

As I emphasized in the introduction, you do not have to give up your zest for achieving excellence just because you have given up your demand for perfection. I have encouraged you to shoot for the stars, and that is exactly what I entreat you to do!

What has gotten you into a perfectionistic habit is not your idealism, but your *misplaced idealism*. It is indeed exciting to aim for an ideal. Living without ideals to strive for can get boring and self-constraining. When you tell yourself the sky is the limit, you can ignite a passion for forward-moving constructive change. It's only when you *demand* that you attain your ideals *perfectly* that you invariably fall short. So I hereby offer you a set of ideals to strive for, with the admonition that you will never perfectly realize them. Like beacons of light, these guiding virtues can guide you to becoming better and better accustomed to emotionally and behaviorally managing the challenges and vicissitudes of everyday living in an imperfect world.

So let's take a look at these guiding virtues that promote the crowning virtue of metaphysical security—these beacons that can guide you from the perils of demanding perfection to getting better at living comfortably in this imperfect world (Cohen, 2007; Cohen, 2017).

Respect

This set of guiding virtues can help us overcome self-destructive tendencies to rate reality, including human reality, as utterly worthless or totally crappy when it's not perfect. Respectful people avoid the irrational tendency to condemn the whole based on the part, and they are open to the inherent goodness in things despite imperfections. There are four types of respect, depending on the object of respect.

UNCONDITIONAL WORLD ACCEPTANCE

This respect avoids damning the world *as a whole* just because it has some negative aspects. Instead, you appreciate that an imperfect world, where there are bad or undesirable things, can still be a good place. So, for example, despite the existence of poverty, sickness, and death, you do not damn the cosmos and are still open to the possibility of good things happening too. Sadly, many people lose sight of the forest for the trees and spend their lives deeply depressed about the crappy things, looking bleakly on the cosmos, and thereby depriving themselves of the opportunity to enjoy the good in the world.

UNCONDITIONAL SELF-ACCEPTANCE

This deep philosophical understanding of human worth and dignity means that you "fully accept yourself even when you perform badly..." and, therefore, "counteracts your self-downing" (Ellis, 2001). To be unconditionally self-accepting means:

- Letting go of your demand for perfection instead of *mus*turbating yourself about being perfect or near-perfect

- Being comfortable with your imperfections

- Distinguishing between the worth of your deeds and your self-worth

- Understanding that making mistakes, doing things that are wrong, or otherwise falling short of your goals does not diminish your value as a person

- Not being afraid to strive for constructive change for fear of failing

- Understanding that failing is part of the process of learning how to improve

UNCONDITIONAL LIFE ACCEPTANCE

You can unconditionally accept yourself without accepting your life, however. "Why do bad things happen to good people?" is a gnawing philosophical question, indeed. The practical starting point is to accept that shit happens. But that doesn't necessarily mean that your life is *totally bad*. "My life sucks, because I deserved to be promoted and instead they promoted that guy who has a fraction of my experience, and now he's my boss." That really is a tough break! But it doesn't mean your life *as a whole* sucks! Unconditional life acceptance means resisting this type of inference and remaining open to the good things in life even when shit happens.

UNCONDITIONAL OTHER ACCEPTANCE

This type of acceptance involves:

- Respecting other people besides yourself, even though they are imperfect and flawed, just like you

- Avoiding damning an entire person because of their shortcomings, misdeeds, or mistakes

- Seeing other people as having inherent worth and dignity in spite of their flaws

"John lied to me, so he's a rotten person" is a self-defeating inference because it leaves no room for rational discussion to resolve the matter. Instead, it fuels blind anger. "In lying to me, John did something rotten" leaves room for rational dialog with John and the possibility of a constructive resolution. Unconditional other acceptance means taking the latter, constructive approach to interpersonal problems.

Authenticity

Authentic people are autonomous (self-determining) and live according to their own creative lights. They therefore do not demand the approval of others in trying to validate themselves. Instead, they value their individuality and personal freedom, and do not attempt to hide their responsibility for their decisions by blaming others or making other lame excuses.

Courage

Being courageous means you are disposed to take reasonable risks, without under- or overestimating the danger. This means being afraid (or not afraid) to the extent that it is reasonable, and acting according to the merits of the situation. The courageous person does not demand certainty before acting but also does not take unreasonable risks. Such a person also does not *awfulize* or *catastrophize* about how bad something is—turning it into the worst thing, or near-worst thing, or much worse than it really is—and then worry excessively about it.

Self-Control

This set of guiding virtues involves *rational* control over your actions, emotions, and will. By telling yourself you *can't* do otherwise, you can defeat your own purposes. For example, you can keep yourself from advancing by refusing to try. In contrast, a person with self-control can take control of her own life (body, mind, and spirit) by cognitively and behaviorally overcoming such self-defeating *can'ts*. There are three type of self-control.

DECISIVENESS

Working toward this guiding virtue builds a habit of realistic trust in your ability to accomplish the goals you set for yourself. Rather than being *can't*stipated by demanding perfection or near-perfection before acting, the decisive person is comfortable with acting under less-than-ideal conditions. For example, human beings are not always able to control what happens, predict the future with accuracy, or know everything before deciding to do something. Decisive people do not procrastinate or otherwise avoid seeking their goals because of such imperfect circumstances. They make rational judgments and act on them.

TOLERANCE AND PATIENCE

These guiding virtues help build your willpower muscle for rationally facing obstacles that frustrate you. The tolerant or patient person avoids the extremes of, on the one hand, weakness of will, and on the other, dogmatic perseverance. For example, a person might tell herself that she *can't stand* a certain person, and then lose control. In contrast, the tolerant or patient person understands the difference between not wanting or choosing whether to stand the person, and not really being able to, and therefore exercises rational constraint in dealing with the person.

TEMPERANCE

This type of self-control involves taking responsibility for your own emotions without making excuses for them. For example, the temperate person is able to avoid extreme, self-defeating emotions such as rage in response to mistreatment by others.

Prudence

Working toward this guiding virtue involves:

- Building a rational understanding of, and tolerance for, the imperfect nature of morality, particularly the inherent ambiguity of making moral decisions

- Cultivating an ability to frame life in constructive, creative ways instead of casting moral choices as hopeless dilemmas ("Damned if I do and damned if I don't") or in black-or-white terms ("Either I succeed or I'm a failure")

- Strengthening the ability to work with others to address problems or disagreements

- Developing the insight to distinguish between what we can change and what we can't, and the ability to work within these limits to make constructive changes, albeit imperfectly

- Becoming a proactive thinker—that is, one disposed to solve problems rather than worry about solving them

Empowerment

To be an empowering person means:

- Being disposed to encourage or inspire others to act as rational, self-determining agents instead of manipulating, deceiving, intimidating, or using power plays to get others to say or do what we want

- Advising rather than goading

- Using rational arguments to convince rather than making threats

- Recognizing the right of others to their own beliefs and values

- Giving others informed consent in matters related to their welfare

Empathy

This habit involves the ability to disregard your own ego-centered universe to connect (cognitively, emotionally, and spiritually) with the subjective views of others to see where they are coming from, even if you don't necessarily agree with them. It means giving up the self-defeating idea that only your own values, interests, preferences, and beliefs are valid.

Objectivity

This is the ability to make unbiased judgments in practical matters. It avoids *oversimplifying reality*, such as:

- Overgeneralizing (for example, "John doesn't like me, so nobody does")

- Pigeonholing (for example, "Either I succeed at this or I'm a failure")

- Stereotyping (for example, "All men cheat")

- Prejudice (for example, "Why was she so unfriendly? I bet she has her period")

Instead, an objective person tends to be:

- Realistic instead of perfectionistic

- Perceptive (seeing more of the nuances of reality rather than a black-or-white vision)

- Open-minded (being open to alternative possibilities)

- Creative (applying of your knowledge base to unfamiliar challenges or situations)

- Constructive (finding rational approaches to problems of living)

Foresightedness

Being foresighted means:

- Checking out the facts before making predictions about the future

- Being aware that certainty is a perfectionistic ideal that does not exist this side of heaven

- Making life decisions and choices based on *probability*, not certainty

- Avoiding catastrophic thinking—that is, not amplifying the risks or consequences of unwanted things happening

Scientific Thinking

In working toward this guiding virtue, you are cultivating a habit of:

- Basing beliefs on evidence rather than on fear or guilt, superstition, magical thinking, wishful thinking, fanaticism, or other antiscientific ways of accounting for reality

- Appreciating that science does not give absolute answers, so beliefs about material reality can always be disconfirmed by future evidence—for example, medical diagnoses can change, for better or worse, depending on further testing or even new technologies

- Having reasonable hope, avoiding pie-in-the-sky optimism on the one hand and dogmatic pessimism on the other

Guiding Virtues Are Interconnected

All of these guiding virtues are interconnected, so that in working toward one of them you are working toward others. For example, in striving to be more decisive, you are likely to become more courageous, because in being more decisive you will be less reluctant to take reasonable risks. As you gain unconditional self-acceptance, you are more likely to also gain authenticity because you will be more self-reliant, as you no longer demand others' approval to validate yourself.

Nevertheless, your choice of the first guiding virtue to work on will depend on what type of perfectionist you are. For example, if you are an achievement perfectionist, then adopting and working on unconditional self-acceptance as your guiding virtue can help you overcome the self-destructive tendency to belittle yourself when you fall short of doing a perfect job. Table 3.1 matches each of the ten types of perfectionism to a set of guiding virtues that includes one or more potent antidotes.

So if, for example, you are an approval perfectionist, then you can overcome your demand for approval by adopting authenticity and unconditional self-acceptance as your guiding virtues and working toward them.

Now, to prepare for this transformative lifelong journey, take a few minutes to complete Exercise 3.1.

EXERCISE 3.1. Identifying Antidotal Habits for Overcoming Your Perfectionism

1. Referring to the results of the self-assessment inventory you recorded in Exercise 2.2, jot down the name of each type of perfectionism you listed.

2. Now, referring to Table 3.1, jot down beside each of these names the set of corresponding guiding virtues for overcoming it.

You have now identified your guiding virtues for overcoming your perfectionism. You will have help in working toward these goals as you study the chapters that cover the specific perfectionism types.

Congratulations! The guiding virtues you have identified are your lifelong aspirations. Indeed, many perfectionists go through a lifetime not even realizing what they need to change in order to live contentedly in an imperfect world. You now have the definite advantage of knowing what to shoot for.

TABLE 3.1. Antidotes to Perfectionism

Type of Perfectionism	Guiding Virtues
Achievement	Unconditional self-acceptance
Approval	Unconditional self-acceptance Authenticity
Moral	Unconditional self-acceptance Courage Prudence
Control	Courage Tolerance/self-control Prudence
Expectation	Unconditional other acceptance Courage Temperance/self-control
Ego-Centered	Empathy Tolerance/self-control Objectivity
Treatment	Courage Prudence Patience
Existential	Unconditional life acceptance Unconditional world acceptance Scientific thinking
Neatness	Unconditional world acceptance Tolerance/self-control
Certainty	Foresightedness Scientific thinking Decisiveness/self-control

Help from the Sages

As briefly discussed in the introduction, great thinkers throughout history have provided incredibly potent and uplifting wisdom for overcoming various types of perfectionism. As you will see, these great ideas can help you build a plan of action for working toward your guiding virtues, and, consequently, replacing your self-destructive perfectionistic habits with constructive ones. In this section we'll look at some helpful examples.

Don't Treat Yourself, or Others, Like Objects

The eighteenth-century German philosopher Immanuel Kant admonishes us not to treat persons, whether ourselves or others, like objects. How do we treat people as objects? We use them, and when they are no longer useful, we discard them! For instance, when that pen of yours runs dry, you think it's useless, throw it away, and get a new one, right? But people are not objects to be used for this or that purpose and discarded when no longer useful. Unlike objects, people have the ability to rationally decide for themselves how they want to be treated. This incredible capacity for rational self-determination gives you (as well as other human beings) an unconditional worth and dignity that clearly distinguishes you from a mere object.

Now, this distinction between persons and objects can be incredibly important in helping to increase unconditional self- and other-acceptance—which, as Table 3.1 indicates, are antidotal habits for overcoming several different types of perfectionism.

Avoid the Extremes; Practice Moderation

Another helpful sage is the ancient Greek philosopher and scientist Aristotle. One key idea he emphasized was moderation, neither overdoing nor underdoing things. When you go to extremes, you typically end up regretting it. For example, when people act rashly without thinking things through, they generally do something foolish—and later regret it. Yet if they are too afraid to act, they generally end up regretting that, too. But when people avoid these extremes, they act *courageously*.

Unfortunately, many perfectionists go to the extreme of demanding perfection before acting (for example, requiring certainty or exaggerating the dangers of acting) and therefore defeat their own purposes. Similarly, people who do not obey moderation regarding their emotions generally end up in deep doo-doo. For example, instead of exercising *temperance* in managing their anger, people who demand perfection of others often self-sabotage by getting too angry when others fall short of their unrealistic expectations.

Aristotle regarded those who avoid the extremes and practice moderation as practically wise, or *prudent*. Such a person, said Aristotle, is "able to deliberate well about what...sorts of thing conduce to the good life in general" (Aristotle, 1941, bk. 6, ch. 5). So, for example, the mom who demands that nothing bad ever happen to her kids, who spends her life worrying about such bad possibilities, does not reason well about how to achieve the good life, for she ends up messing up her own life as well as her kids' lives!

Take Responsibility for Your Emotions

As discussed in the introduction, the ancient Stoic philosopher Epictetus is known for observing that it's not the events in your life that upset you, but what you tell yourself about those events (Epictetus, 1948). Unfortunately, many perfectionists tend to deny their responsibility in upsetting themselves by using language that denies their responsibility, such as:

- "Getting that speeding ticket *made me depressed.*"

- "That son-of-a-bitch *really pissed me off.*"

- "Having to wait in line all that time *made me anxious.*"

- "Thinking I might get fired is *driving me crazy!*"

How about saying instead that you are depressing yourself, pissing yourself off, making yourself anxious, and driving yourself crazy?

You Freely Define Yourself by Acting

Jean-Paul Sartre states that you freely define who you become through your actions (Sartre, 1989). So the perfectionist who is reticent to act, because she is afraid she won't be perfect, defeats her own purpose through inaction by defining herself negatively—as nothing at all. If instead she stands up to her angst and acts, even though she won't be perfect, she defines herself positively as being courageous. We might well paraphrase Sartre's admonition to the anxious perfectionist as "You can run, but you can't hide!"

It's Time: Taking Positive Steps Toward Overcoming Your Perfectionism

I hope you are excited about embarking on this journey toward greater metaphysical security! What makes it most exciting is that there is always room for improvement in building excellence. Much like striving to be a fine virtuoso, the sky is the limit! It therefore entails a lifelong commitment to working on becoming better and better. *But not perfect!* You will never be perfectly respectful, self-controlling, authentic, prudent, objective, empathetic, foresighted, or empowering. But with work, you can improve, more and more, and consequently experience less and less stress generated from an endless roller-coaster ride of *mus*turbation.

Are you ready to make the commitment? If so, then you are ready to proceed to the chapters in this book that tackle your specific types of perfectionism. Which of these chapters should you read first? I suggest you begin with those that deal with the types of perfectionism for which you have the greatest proclivity. Go to your journal and check your responses to Exercise 2.2—the tendency column for each of the types of perfectionism you listed. These tendencies are Almost always, Often, Sometimes. Start with the perfectionism type (or types) for which you recorded the greatest tendency.

I look forward to working with you!

CHAPTER 4

Achievement Perfectionism

Achievement perfectionists make absolutist demands on themselves, for example, that they must:

- Never, or almost never, make any mistakes, even very small inconsequential ones

- Always or almost always meet their goals, or at least certain goals

- Always or almost always be the best at everything, or at least at certain things

- Always or almost always do flawless, or near flawless, work or deeds

These demands are either impossible or nearly impossible to satisfy in this imperfect world. As such, achievement perfectionists tend to set themselves up for failure and then torment themselves for having failed to meet their self-imposed demands. This can be an incredibly stressful way to live.

When Achievement Makes or Breaks Your Self-Worth

Achievement perfectionists define their worth as human beings in terms of their achievements. When they accomplish the tasks by which they define their self-worth, they think themselves worthy. When they are not so achieving, they sink into a dogmatic denouncement of their worth (and therefore their dignity or self-respect), not just as workers or professionals but also as human beings.

Loss of Creativity

This type of self-regarding perfectionism is prevalent in very creative people. So you may be in good company! The bad news is that it can stifle the very creativity you seek to express. A telling example is the case of creative writers who experience writer's block. According to one study of thirty-three blocked writers, all of them exhibited depression and anxiety, including symptoms of self-doubt and perfectionism (Kaufman, 2009). Having defined their self-worth in term of the ability to write, these writers experienced strong self-doubts when they were unable to write. The more prolonged their inability, the more they sank into the hopelessness of depression. But maybe everything was cool when these creative folks were successfully producing good writing? Wrong! In fact, achievement perfectionists are likely to be in a state of constant anxiety, whether or not they are producing good prose. They never know when the productivity might come to a screeching halt.

Anxiety Takes Its Toll

Such ongoing, intense anxiety can take its toll. I have heard ad nauseam from many doctoral students preparing for work as philosophy professors about how they could not imagine what they would do with their lives if they were never able to land a job as a philosophy professor. These deeply committed individuals conceived their self-worth largely in terms of teaching philosophy full time, so they could not even imagine how they could survive the harsh (yet very real) possibility of never being able to devote their life to what they were trained to do. As a result, they suffered intense anxiety.

Mired in Catastrophic Thoughts

I have also worked with many undergraduate students who were psychologically in the same boat. Often, it was in the pursuit of that "perfect" 4.0 average. "I *must* get an A in your class, Dr. Cohen." If I had a dollar for every student who's told me this, I would have retired to Tahiti long ago. For many of these students, the very thought of getting a "B" was utter desolation—it meant being an irredeemable failure! Many athletes are of the same mind, in my experience. As long as they are doing well in their sport, they are flying high, but lurking beneath the thin veneer of temporary success is the daunting, ever-present possibility of screwing up on the field or court and thereby falling into the dreaded depths of despair.

Offending Others

Some high achievers may also demand omniscience—that is, perfect or near-perfect knowledge of the universe. These people experience strong anxiety when they are unable to answer a question or they get the answer wrong. Some are obsessed with asking questions to ensure that nothing slips by them. They often have difficulty with interpersonal relationships because others perceive them as insisting on knowing personal information. Sadly, such individuals are often very insecure and experience intense self-doubts when they think there is something they don't know.

Loss of Productivity

Some achievement demanders may be so mired in doing a perfect or near-perfect job that their work output suffers dramatically. A very talented attorney spent so much time preparing each brief that he was not able to accommodate his workload and meet deadlines, and ultimately he lost his position. For this dedicated perfectionist, his work product *had* to be a work of art before he gave it the green light. Balancing quality with productivity was not something this poor fellow was willing to try, and he ended up achieving neither.

Afraid to Try

Achievement perfectionism can also manifest itself in underachieving populations as well as those motivated to overachieve. For example, I have had students as well as clients who were afraid to try to succeed because they feared that they would fail, which was worse than actually trying and failing. They never excelled in anything because they never even tried to do so, despite their often strong potential for doing good work.

Exercise 4.1 should help you begin to think more carefully about achievement perfectionism and how it may be affecting your life.

EXERCISE 4.1. Your Issues Related to Achievement Perfectionism

Consider the following questions and write your responses in your journal.

- *Can you identify with any of the examples of achievement perfection- ists I have discussed? If so, in what respect/s?*

- *Are you ever anxious about the possibility of failing, making a mistake, or otherwise not being perfect or near-perfect? If so, how often?*

- *Do you ever experience depression over having failed, made a mistake, or otherwise not been perfect or near-perfect? If so, how often?*

- *Does the possibility of failing keep you from trying to do new things? If so, how often?*

- *Are you presently experiencing any work-related or personal prob- lems? If so, do you think they may have something to do with achieve- ment perfectionism? If so, in what way/s?*

The frequency of the issues you have described should also give you an idea of how often achievement perfectionism may be undermining your peace and prosperity.

Achievement Perfectionism Feeds Low Self-Esteem

Achievement perfectionists often use the things they have done wrong to prove to themselves that they really are unworthy; many are often also hard on others when they mess up (Muoio, 2015). Some achievement demanders experience self-doubt even when they perform well and others are impressed. These individuals often focus on their imperfections and believe that they have merely deceived others into thinking they are worthy. Some of them are decisive in the presence of others, even when they make mistakes, while others wear their self-doubts on their shirt-sleeves. So how do you manage your self-doubts? Take some time to reflect on the questions in Exercise 4.2.

EXERCISE 4.2. How Do You Manage Your Self-Doubt?

Reflect on the following questions and enter your answers in your journal.

- *Do you ever experience self-doubt when you make mistakes, even small ones? If so, describe a situation when you felt this way. What are you telling yourself about yourself?*

- *What do you do in a social context—making a presentation, per-forming, making a speech, or even speaking to a group of friends, coworkers, or peers—when you make a mistake: stumble on words, lose your trend of thought, play a sour note, or not know an answer to a question?*

    - *Do you feel self-conscious and keep ruminating about it?*

    - *Do you try to hide your self-doubt?*

    - *Do you let others know how you are feeling on the inside?*

- *Do you ever look for something you have done wrong, thinking that there must be something? If so, give an example.*

- *Do you ever feel like you are putting one over on others who are impressed with you because you are sure they have not really dis-covered yet just how flawed you really are? If so, how often? In what sorts of situations?*

Telling yourself that you are an unworthy person who manages to trick others is self-defeating because even if you achieve your goal (for example, get through a presentation successfully), you will have needlessly upset yourself and deprived yourself of the satisfaction of successfully completing a task. On the other hand, sharing your self-doubts indis-criminately with others when you make a mistake ("I feel like such an idiot") is also self-defeating because you undermine your own dignity by inviting others not to take you seriously. In each case, the root of the problem is the same: defining your self-worth in terms of whether you satisfy your unrealistic demand to be perfect or near-perfect.

What steps can you take to overcome this self-defeating, stressful habit? Fortunately, we can apply the six-step method discussed in the introduction!

Step 1: Identify Your Irrational Thinking

Here are the *premises* behind the faulty logic of the achievement perfectionist:

1. I must not make mistakes.

2. Therefore, if I make a mistake, it will mean I'm worthless/a failure/a screw-up.

3. I've made a mistake, failed, or otherwise fallen short.

4. Therefore, I'm worthless/a failure/a screw-up.

Notice how the "must" in premise 1 is at the root of your needless stress. If you *must* not make mistakes, then *if* you fail to measure up, you *are* the failure, the screw-up, or the worthless heap of garbage. It is this "if" in premise 2 that creates your anxiety, because anxiety is always about what might happen in the future *if* something goes wrong. So even if you haven't yet messed up, you are still going to be anxious about this possibility happening in the future. After all, *if* you do mess up, then you are relegated to being worthless crap. So the part of your brain that makes practical decisions (the neocortex) sends a danger signal to your amygdala, which signals other parts of your brain (such as your hypothalamus) to prepare your body for the danger, which, as you have seen, also reduces your ability to think clearly. Now it becomes more likely that you *will* mess up (so that permise 3 comes true), which in turn leads you to conclude that you are indeed that pile of trash (see premise 4).

It should now be evident how you can defeat your own purposes and cause yourself a whole lot of stress by buying into the "must" in premise 1. Once you accept it, it's all downhill from there!

Let's get clear about your own premises with Exercise 4.3.

EXERCISE 4.3. Identify Your Self-Disturbing Thinking

1. Think about something you believe you have recently done wrong, some perceived failing, mistake, or shortcoming that you have been really down on yourself about. Try to describe this thing you think you've done wrong in as few words as possible in your journal. Also write down how you are negatively rating yourself for having done this thing, and sum it up in a few words, such as "a failure," "a screw-up," or whatever best captures your own self-downing language.

2. Now enter the brief description of your action and the rating of yourself in this reasoning template. Enter the filled-out template in your journal.

    1. I must never [*what you did that you are down on yourself about*].

    1. Therefore, if I [*what you did*], then I am a [*your negative rating*].

    2. I have done what I must never do.

    1. Therefore, I am a [*your negative self-rating*].

This filled-in reasoning template is the actual thought process by which you berate and disturb yourself! Keep it handy as you work through the rest of this chapter.

Step 2: Refute Your Irrational Premises

Now you are in a position to see just why your achievement perfectionism rests on irrational premises. This will entail two substeps.

Refute Your *Must*

Stopping your *musturbation*—letting go of the *must* in premise 1—is clearly the key to giving up your habit of achievement perfectionism. And here is one good reason why your demand for perfection can be *refuted*: if you or any other human person *must* not make mistakes, or at least not stupid ones, then none of us would ever make them, because if something must not be, it just doesn't happen! But of course we all make mistakes, even stupid ones! That should be enough to show you that your *must* is contrary to the facts, and therefore plainly irrational.

Refute Your Self-Damnation

You should now see that the "must" in premise 1 is irrational. But old habits are not easily broken, and I suspect you are still inclined to damn yourself when you mess up. So let's refute premise 2: if you screw up, then you are a screw-up. Ponder this bit of logical wisdom: "What's true of the part is not necessarily true of the whole." Suppose you have blue eyes. That does not mean that *you* are blue. Likewise, just because you made a mistake, failed at something, or did something that was inferior or second rate does not mean that *you* are a mistake, a failure, inferior, or second rate. You might as well conclude that you are blue! Indeed, inasmuch as we are all imperfect, we all screw up—which, according to this twisted logic, would mean that we are all screw-ups. This is plainly absurd!

Step 3: Identify Your Guiding Virtues

Because you define your self-worth in terms of whether you are achieving your goals, your ability to accept yourself is very fragile and conditional. As such, the guiding virtue for overcoming this tendency is *unconditional self-acceptance*. So how can you become more unconditionally self-accepting?

Step 4: Gain Philosophical Wisdom from the Sages

As discussed in Chapter Three, "Self-respect involves *unconditional self-acceptance* based upon a deep philosophical understanding of human worth and dignity" (Cohen, 2007, 17). Philosophers since antiquity have pontificated about the basis of human worth and dignity:

Exercise your ability to reason. "You are a rational animal. It is your ability to think and reason that separates you from other species of animals" (Aristotle, 1941).

Treat yourself as a person, not an object: "You are not a mere object but instead a person with the ability to rationally determine your own life" (Kant, 1964).

Freely make plans and act on them: Jean-Paul Sartre reminds us that, unlike mosses or cauliflowers, we are conscious, self-aware beings who have a subjective life and can freely make plans and act on them. An anecdote from Sartre drives home the point: When he was imprisoned, he met a Jesuit priest who had grown up in poverty; was degraded by his schoolmates; had a grievous, failed relationship at eighteen; and failed his military exam. Sartre explains that this man could have regarded himself as a "total failure" but instead took his bad luck as a sign that he was meant for the clergy. "[T]he decision was his and his alone," Sartre declared, for he could just as easily have become a carpenter or revolutionary (Sartre, 1989).

So it's really your choice if you want to proclaim *yourself* a failure when you can just as well see not being successful at something in a positive light. After all, you hold the reins over your own subjectivity and can be as creative as you wish. So think twice before you treat yourself like some inert piece of garbage. You've got free will, so use it!

Step 5: Build a Rational Plan of Action

I urge you to heed the advice of our sages by treating yourself with the self-respect that you deserve. As you can see, unconditional self-acceptance is not about being perfect or imperfect. *Human nature is imperfect, but you have admirable capacities for reason, self-determination, and subjectivity that ground unconditionally treating yourself with respect.*

This is going to take work—in particular, developing a plan of action for making constructive changes, and then acting on it. So let's get started!

What Are You Doing Now?

In helping my clients formulate a plan of action to overcome self-defeating habits, I first ask them what they generally *do* when they find they have fallen short of their unrealistic, perfectionistic demand. Some common responses are:

- I keep to myself or avoid others.

- I try to self-medicate with drugs or alcohol.

- I stay up at night ruminating about it.

- I sit in my office ruminating about it, or leave work early.

These behaviors are the self-destructive results of demanding perfection and then damning yourself when you don't achieve it. This is how you punish and degrade yourself for your perceived failure.

Ask the Sages

What might the philosophers tell you to do instead of what you are doing? Would a sage tell you to torment yourself as you do, going through the antics of rumination, isolating yourself, keeping yourself up all night, self-medicating, and so forth? Clearly not!

ARISTOTLE

Think rationally, exercise self-control, and act accordingly. Aristotle would *not* prescribe avoiding others. Instead, he might tell you to do what you enjoy doing, because there is no rational sense in punishing yourself by locking yourself away. After all, it is not a crime to be human! And no doubt self-medicating would not be on Aristotle's list of to-dos; that would impair your ability to think rationally and would not solve a damn thing. He would recommend:

- Fake it until you make it. Constructive change is possible only through practice.

- Socialize with others. Aristotle said that we humans are "social animals"!

- Exercise rational self-control rather than pine away. This is how you can become virtuous.

- If you feel like avoiding others, try to be especially outgoing instead. You'll end up being not outgoing, but rather just more sociable.

KANT

Stop treating yourself like an object that has malfunctioned and instead treat yourself with unconditional worth and dignity. This involves exercising your self-determination. Instead of ruminating about what a failure you are, exercise that willpower muscle of yours to do something that you enjoy or that is constructive. He would recommend:

- Do something rational, like reading a good book or whatever other rational activity floats your boat. Kant believed that you should not let your reason become a slave to your emotions.

- Don't call yourself nasty names, degrade yourself to others, or otherwise put yourself down. That's no way to respect yourself as a person.

- Distract yourself with something you enjoy doing, like eating your favorite dessert, listening to your favorite music, or watching an upbeat movie. You would rationally wish that others treat themselves well; be consistent in treating yourself the same.

SARTRE

Like the man in Sartre's story, you have the freedom to interpret your situation as you choose. Sartre would therefore remind you that your demand for perfection exists only because you have decided it does, and that if you choose to ruminate or otherwise torture and degrade yourself about having made a mistake or failed at something, then you bear the responsibility for it. It's your choice, and you are free to move on with your life. Think positive. You have the power! Sartre would recommend:

- Reframe your experience as a learning experience.

- Give yourself permission to be a fallible human; it is part of the human condition to make mistakes and fail.

- Do something you always wanted to do but never found the time to do—for example, sign up for music or dance lessons. You can define yourself only through action, not by talking about what you coulda, shoulda done.

Now it's time to put that power to work by creating and implementing your own plan of action. Exercise 4.4 will help you do just that!

EXERCISE 4.4. Create Your Plan of Action

1. Identify your behavioral responses. Think again about the perceived mistake or failing you've been working through in the previous exercises. Now make a list of the ways you responded behaviorally to this situation (say, you avoided others, ruminated, kept yourself up at night thinking about it, or were discouraged to pursue new opportunities).

2. Create your plan of action. What would each of our sages tell you to do differently? Based on these insights, make another creative list of things you would do differently. *This list will be your plan of action!*

Step 6: Put Your Plan of Action into Practice

Now it's time to implement your plan of action. This is where you can begin to build a habit of unconditional self-acceptance to replace your tendency to damn yourself when you fall short of your perfectionistic demand. This is where you begin to *emotionally* accept the fact that you are a fallible human being like the rest of us! Chapter Fourteen, "Putting Your Action Plan to Work," will get you started. As you work through the exercises in that chapter and begin building your new skills in making peace with your achievement imperfections, keep these three key ideas in mind:

- If I *must* be perfect, or near-perfect, then how come no one else is?

- Human nature is imperfect, but I have admirable capacities for reason, self-determination, and subjectivity that support unconditionally treating myself with respect.

- If making mistakes diminished my worthiness as a person, we'd all be unworthy.

If you have other types of imperfection to make peace with, feel free to continue with the type-specific chapters that follow—but first work through Exercises 14.1 and 14.2, so you are familiar with the all-important final step of the method.

CHAPTER 5

Approval Perfectionism

People who are approval perfectionists may:

- Experience strong self-doubt when they don't get the approval of at least certain people

- Feel they must be liked, loved, or approved of by *everyone* (or almost everyone) and experience self-doubts when that doesn't happen

- Go out of their way to make sure others like, love, or approve of them, even to the point of doing things that they think are wrong or that are very inconvenient

- Worry for extended periods about not having or getting the approval of others

As mentioned in Chapter Two, this type of self-regarding perfectionism involves *demanding* that you be loved, liked, or approved of by at least certain others. Now, you may be thinking, "Doesn't everyone want to be approved of by peers, friends, family, coworkers, and so on? Isn't it just natural to want to be accepted?" And you have a point. Of course, we all would prefer to be liked, loved, or approved of by others, and most of us would welcome it. But this is not the same thing as *demanding* approval, and it is precisely this demand that makes approval perfectionism self-destructive. The world we inhabit is not an ideal one where we always get what we want or prefer. So, while it can be preferable, even desirable, that others like, love, approve of, or otherwise accept you, it is unrealistic to demand it.

The Definition of Approval Perfectionism

Let's first take a careful look at this demand for approval. There are two related demands that can easily be confused:

1. *I* must get the approval of others.

2. *Others* must approve of me.

Notice that the second one makes a demand on *others*, while the first makes a demand on *oneself*. As we will discuss in Chapter Nine, the second demand is a type of ego-centered perfectionism. In contrast, approval demanders are in a habit of making the first demand on themselves. If you don't get the approval of others (or certain others), you experience self-doubt. You perceive your self-worth in terms of whether *you succeed* at getting the approval of others. You tell yourself that you must get this approval in order to be a worthy human being, so you put a lot of pressure on yourself to obtain this approval, which can leave you in a constant state of anxiety about whether you will succeed in getting and maintaining it. Moreover, cases in which you do not successfully obtain or maintain the approval you demand can leave you feeling depressed or down about yourself. Not exactly the way to live a peaceful life!

Further, let's be clear about the object of the approval you are demanding. As a demander of approval, your bottom line is to successfully secure others' approval of *you as a person*. Such approval of *you* is distinct from approval of *what you say or do*. These objects of approval are distinct, because others can approve of you as a person even though they don't approve of your conduct, and vice versa. However, to get and maintain others' approval of you, ordinarily it's also necessary to get others to approve of the things you say or do. Consequently, approval perfectionists typically place a further demand on themselves: to get others to approve of the things they say or do. For example, suppose you demand that your colleague, whom you respect, approve of you as a person. If you think you said something with which he disagrees, you may in turn be anxious that he may stop approving of you. Here you may be demanding of yourself that you not say anything with which your colleague might disagree, so you can continue to maintain your colleague's approval.

So, essentially, *approval perfectionism* entails:

1. Demanding that you get and maintain others' approval of you as a person

2. Demanding that you say or do things that get and maintain others' approval of you as a person

3. Evaluating your self-worth on the basis of whether or not you get and maintain others' approval of you as a person

There are at least four common ways in which approval perfectionists try to satisfy the second characteristic. To get and maintain others' approval, you may:

- Dedicate yourself to impressing others

- Try to control things perfectly or near-perfectly

- Conform blindly to or imitate others

- Let yourself be exploited by others

Let's look at each of these.

Dedicating Yourself to Impressing Others

I have counseled individuals who have spent much of their lives trying to gain their parents' approval. Many have been high achievers yet could never seem to do enough to satisfy their parents. One earned a PhD in physics, became a professor, and rose to the rank of dean at his university. Still, his father never approved of him as a person. So this poor fellow continued to think of himself as second rate, and not really deserving of his professional status. There was no question that he had achieved great things. But it all meant nothing to him, because his father never acknowledged any of it but instead continued to belittle and find fault with him. The dean demanded of himself that he achieve things that would win his father's approval, but he never seemed (in his mind) to get it right. It was not until he realized that he was demanding his father's approval of him as a person, and that this unrequited demand was the source of his self-doubt, that he began to make progress in therapy.

Controlling the Situation

Many approval perfectionists try to control the situation in order to get and maintain others' approval. They try to prevent anything from happening that has a chance of leading to their not getting or losing that approval. This was the case with one of my former clients, Bob, who worked in an in-patient facility as a psychiatric nurse. He told me that each evening after work he would experience intense anxiety thinking about the next day at work.

"I *must* be in control of the situation at work at all times," declared Bob.

"And what would happen if you weren't always in control?" I asked.

"Something bad might happen to one of my patients on my watch."

"And what would be the significance of that happening?"

"It would mean that I'm a loser!"

"Why would that make you a loser?"

"Because my boss would lose respect for me."

"So you must have your boss's respect; and if you lose it, you're a loser?"

"Yes!"

As you can see, Bob's demand for control was based on his demand for his boss's approval—in particular, for his respect. He demanded control at all times at work so that he wouldn't make any mistakes that could cost him his boss's approval. Indeed, in his judgment this would have rendered him unworthy as a person, "a loser." Only when Bob began to appreciate that his self-worth did not depend on his boss's approval of him as a person did he begin to make progress in overcoming his anxiety.

Conforming to or Imitating Others

Here are some common ways people conform to or imitate others to get their approval.

The Blind Conformist

Many approval perfectionists are conformity junkies; that is, they feel compelled to do things just to fit in. This can be a perilous existence, because you may be willing to do things that are self-destructive just to gain the approval of others. Take the case of my high school friend Larry. He had speech impediments: a lisp and a stutter. Other students often mocked him about it, which led Larry to question his self-worth and to think of himself as a social outcast, a reject or loser. After graduation, trying to fit in, Larry befriended a group of high-risk-takers who would go drag racing down the narrow, winding roads of Upper Saddle River, New Jersey. Sadly, one evening Larry was ejected from the back seat of a speeding car when it struck a tree. The driver and the passenger who sat up front were killed instantly, but Larry remained in a coma for a few months in a nursing home until he finally passed away. I often think about Larry and his plight. He was a kind, generous spirit who had the capacity to live a fulfilling life, but instead chose to take unreasonable risks in order to gain the approval of a misguided lot. Larry demanded of himself that he gain the approval of this group, and, at just eighteen, paid for it with his life.

The Dependent Lover

Some approval demanders also take conformity to the extreme of giving up their individuality in order to be accepted by others. This often occurs in dysfunctional relationships. Some people perceive themselves as incomplete unless they have a spouse or partner beside them. For example, writing about dependent love in heterosexual women, philosopher Simone de Beauvoir observes, "the supreme happiness of the woman in love is to be recognized by the loved man as a part of himself..."; and when she is without a man, she is, in the words of Cecile Sauvage, "a scattered bouquet" (de Beauvoir, 2000, 138). Here such dependent individuals (which can also include same-sex couples) think they *must* have the love of a partner or they are nothing.

The Displaced Homemaker

When death or divorce separates such ⌐
partners, they are left without a purpose in
group of displaced middle-aged homemake
Before they could move forward, they need
determination, an awareness that they had the ability ⌐ ⌐
independent purposes. This was very frightening for most of them, but ⌐y
relinquishing the idea that they must have such dependent love of another
to be worthy as persons, they were able to take constructive steps to liber-
ate themselves from a self-stultifying, self-imposed form of bondage.
Pushing back against this inertia, some began to build a new life for themselves by going back to school, learning new skills, and seeking gainful
employment outside the home.

Letting Yourself Be Exploited by Others

Still other approval demanders let themselves be exploited by others in
order to get and maintain their approval. These people allow others to
take advantage of them, sometimes even to the point of tolerating their
abuse. For example, in an office environment they may perform menial
tasks or things nobody else wants to do in order to gain or maintain the
approval of their peers. They are often first to volunteer for tasks they
would have preferred not to do. They tend to have a hard time saying no
because they fear rejection by others. As a result, they are easily taken
advantage of by others.

What Are Your Approval-Seeking Ways?

Exercise 5.1 can help you get clearer about your own ways of seeking
approval.

5.1. How Do You Try to Get Others' ʌroval?

ʌhink about the following questions and write down your responses in your journal.

- *What sort of things do you do to try to get and maintain others' approval of you as a person? Do you conform? Try to impress others? Control the situation? Let yourself be exploited? In what ways?*

- *Do you take yet another approach?*

- *Can you identify with any of the examples of approval perfectionists discussed in this chapter? If so, in what respect/s?*

- *How do you feel when you think you have lost, or may not get, the approval of someone whose approval you demand?*

Keeping your responses to Exercise 5.1 in mind, it's now time to work on overcoming your approval perfectionism, using the six-step method described in the introduction.

Step 1: Identify Your Irrational Thinking

Let's look carefully at the thinking that drives approval perfectionism:

1. I must get others' approval of me as a person.

2. Therefore, if I don't get this approval, I'll be a reject or loser.

3. If I don't impress/control/conform/let myself be exploited, I won't get this approval.

4. Therefore, if I don't impress/control/conform/let myself be exploited, I'll be a reject or loser.

5. Therefore, I must impress/control/conform/let myself be exploited.

As you can see, it's your perfectionistic demand for approval in premise 1 that leads you to experience self-doubt about ending up a social outcast—a "reject" or "loser." This is the root of your anxiety about your future status, which leads you to resort to such tactics as impressing others, conforming, controlling, or letting yourself be exploited to head off not getting that self-affirming approval, which would make you a reject or loser. So you conclude that you *must* resort to at least one of these tactics (or something like it), or be relegated to the lowly status of reject or loser.

EXERCISE 5.2. Identify Your Self-Disturbing Thinking

1. Think again about the ways you try to get and maintain others' approval, which you jotted down in Exercise 5.1, Try to sum these up in as few words as possible (for example, "flatter/brag/do what others expect"). Also write down how you negatively rate yourself when you do not get this approval or think you may not get it, and sum it up in a word or two, such as "reject," "loser," or whatever best captures your own self-degrading language.

2. Now enter the brief description and your self-rating in this reasoning template. Enter the filled-in template in your journal. This is the actual thought process by which you disturb yourself!

   1. I must get others' approval of me as a person.

   2. So, if I don't get this approval, then I'll be a [*your negative self-rating*].

   3. If I don't [*what you do for approval*], I won't get this approval.

   4. So, if I don't [*what you do for approval*], I'll be a [*your negative self-rating*].

   5. So I must [*what you do for approval*].

Keep this filled-in thinking template handy as you work through the rest of this chapter.

Step 2: Refute Your Irrational Premises

Unfortunately, your thinking rests on irrational premises. Let's start by debunking the "must" in premise 1.

Refute Your *Must*

If it were really true that you *must* have others' approval, as premise 1 demands, then you would always have it, automatically. Yes, automatically, because "must" means "necessarily," and whatever is necessary cannot possibly *not* be. But you don't always get others' approval. So your *must*urbatory demand is irrational.

Refute Your Self-Damnation

As for premise 2, it is also irrational. Does your self-worth really depend on getting the approval of others? *Well, in that case, many people who did great things would also be rejects and losers.* For example, Galileo, now considered the father of modern science, was condemned by the church as a heretic and spent the last decade of his life under house arrest. Had Galileo given a damn about what the church thought of him, we all might have been the worse for it!

Step 3: Identify Your Guiding Virtues

On your journey toward greater self-security in a world where not everyone must always approve of you, here are two healthy goals you can adopt instead.

Unconditional Self-Acceptance

In demanding the approval of others to validate your worth and dignity as a person, you turn yourself into an object, a mere means to gain the approval of others. However, in aspiring to be *unconditionally* self-accepting, you can begin to overcome this self-degrading habit.

Authenticity

Your approval perfectionism can also lead to loss of authenticity because it can lead to loss of your:

- Sense of right and wrong

- Personal values

- Self-respect

- Sense of freedom

- Self-determination

So my young friend Larry's approval perfectionism obscured his sense of right and wrong, and it cost him his life. The good college dean assessed his accomplishments based on whether or not his father was impressed, so he could not develop an independent, authentic assessment of his own accomplishments. People who allow themselves to be exploited by others render themselves nonautonomous; the dependent lover suffers a loss of independent self. Clearly, all could have benefited from becoming more authentic in confronting their life challenges!

Step 4: Gain Philosophical Wisdom from the Sages

To develop unconditional self-acceptance, Aristotle says, "Love yourself"— by treating yourself as your own best friend (Aristotle, 1941, bk. 9, ch. 8). Now, would your best friend call you a loser or a reject if you performed poorly or didn't gain the approval of others? No! Instead, she might encourage you to do things you can take pride in doing, not to get the approval of others but for their own sake. For example, you could be friendly, fair, and helpful to others; or, if others were being unfair or rude to you, you could deal with them in a firm, rational manner—thereby shifting your focus from trying to get others to approve of you, as a person, to taking pride in doing praiseworthy things for their own sake.

To become more authentic, Friedrich Nietzsche says, "Create your own values." This nineteenth-century German existentialist was among the most ardent defenders of authentic existence in the history of thought. "The noble kind of man," said Nietzsche, "experiences himself as a person who determines value and does not need to have other people's approval.... He understands himself as something which in general first confers honor on things, as someone who creates values" (Nietzsche, 1954, sec. 260, 579). This involves looking at things in the opposite way you have been accustomed to looking at them. Instead of being a member of a docile herd, a virtual slave to others who seek to exploit you for their own self-aggrandizement, you can be a master. *You* can decide for yourself what is good or bad, right or wrong! Of course, this is an ideal, and you will never attain it perfectly, but aspiring to be such a "superman" (as Nietzsche calls it) can be an excellent antidote to making yourself dependent on the approval of others for self-validation.

Step 5: Build a Rational Plan of Action

What are you doing now? How do you try to enlist others' approval of you as a person? These will be the things you listed in Exercise 5.1, such as conforming to what is expected of you, even when you feel uncomfortable about it.

What Would the Sages Tell You to Do Differently?

Aristotle would definitely not tell you to squander your happiness trying to get others' approval, because *you would not be your best friend if you treated yourself like that.* Indeed, for Aristotle, the approval of others would not be the end goal. He might suggest that you:

- Rationally assess the merits of your actions. ("It's irrational to go against my beliefs or better judgment, just to get others' approval.")

- Do good deeds because you believe them to be good. ("I'll do it, not to impress you, but because it's the right thing.")

- Accept the limitations on what is in your power to control. ("I can control my own emotions, but I can't control yours.")

- Respectfully but firmly decline to do what others can appropriately do for themselves. ("This is not part of my job description.")

Nietzsche would encourage you to *turn your approval perfectionism on its head*:

- Set an example for others to follow. ("It can be exciting to be innovative rather than to be part of the herd.")

- Let others try to impress you. ("I am not impressed by the way my dad tries to put me down.")

- Accept the inherent uncertainty of human existence. ("It's absurd to think I can control everything.")

- Oppose those who try to exploit you. ("I am not going to be someone's slave!")

EXERCISE 5.3. Create Your Plan of Action

1. Identify your behavioral responses. Look carefully at the ways you try to get and maintain others' approval that you jotted down in Exercise 5.1. (For example, "I try to make people I really respect think that I am just like them by telling them all the things we have in common. Sometimes I even make things up to impress them.")

2. Create your plan of action. Based on the insights from Aristotle and Nietzsche, make another creative list of the things you would do differently. *This new list will be your plan of action!*

Add a Shame-Attacking Exercise!

While you are working on your plan of action, it can be helpful to intentionally stage a situation in which others may be negatively judging you (Ellis & Grieger, 1977). For example:

- Walk down a crowded street pulling a banana on a string (Albert Ellis suggested this one!).

- Start up a conversation with a waitress you don't know about something that never happened (I did this one when I trained in REBT).

- Dine in a busy, upscale restaurant by yourself while wearing a suit and a hat with a giant picture of a roach on it.

Or, just use your imagination! Three caveats, however: it should not be illegal, immoral, or dangerous.

Step 6: Put Your Plan of Action into Practice

It's now time to implement your plan of action. This is where you can begin to work toward your guiding virtues of unconditional self-acceptance and authenticity and begin to *emotionally* accept the fact that you do not need others' approval to be a worthy person. Here are three key ideas to keep in mind when you put your action plan into practice:

- If my self-worth depended on others' approval of me as a person, many of the greatest benefactors of humanity would be rejects and losers.

- In demanding the approval of others, I turn myself into the slave of others.

- What kind of best friend am I to torment and degrade myself over getting someone's approval?

Let's break the ice with Exercise 5.4.

EXERCISE 5.4. Attack Your Shame!

1. Identify a shame-attacking exercise you are willing to do.

2. Make yourself do it even though you feel uncomfortable about it. "But people are going to look at me like there's something wrong with me!" Well, that's the point, but so what? Prove to yourself you don't need their approval by doing it anyway!

3. If you begin to feel ashamed while performing the exercise, just think about those three key ideas, and keep pushing yourself to complete the exercise. No excuses! Just do it!

4. As soon as possible after you finish your shame-attacking exercise, reflect on your experience:

*   *How did you feel when you were doing it?*

*   *How do you feel now?*

*   *You have told yourself that you must have the approval of others. Now consider whether you have again proven this idea false.*

After you have performed your shame-attacking exercise, congratulate yourself, and give yourself a special treat. While you work on the other items in your plan of action, feel free to repeat this exercise as often as you think it would be helpful.

Now that you've limbered up with a shame-attacking exercise, to continue building your new skills in making peace with not always getting others' approval, proceed to Chapter Fourteen. If you have other types of perfectionism to work on, feel free to continue with the other type-specific chapters—but first work through Exercises 14.1 and 14.2, so you are familiar with the all-important final step of the method.

CHAPTER 6

Moral Perfectionism

As stated in Chapter Two, moral perfectionism is a type of self-regarding perfectionism in which you demand that you never, in any way, violate your moral principles. People who are moral perfectionists typically:

- Experience intense guilt when they think they have done something morally wrong, even if it's a very minor moral wrong

- Think they are bad when they believe they have—or simply *might have*—done something morally wrong

- Ruminate about their perceived moral wrongdoing, even very minor instances

- Experience intense anxiety about making moral choices

- Procrastinate about making or acting on hard moral choices

Let's be clear: there is nothing wrong with being a morally self-conscious person. As a moral perfectionist, you seek to do what you think is morally right. You have a set of moral principles or a personal moral code, and you seek to honor it. This is an admirable trait, and you are to be commended for it. However, there is a huge difference between trying to do what is morally right and *demanding* that you always achieve this noble end.

What's Wrong with Demanding Moral Perfection?

Unfortunately, this demand is unrealistic; here's why:

- You are human, which means you are a fallible creature subject to mistakes in judgment.

- Situations may be morally uncertain, ambiguous, or subject to alternative interpretations about what is morally right.

- Conflicts can and often do arise where you cannot possibly meet all of your moral standards.

- The demand for moral perfection is absolute, whereas rational moral duties or obligation permit exceptions.

Being Human

Aristotle defined human beings as rational animals (Aristotle, 1941). We have this incredible ability to reason, but we also have an emotional "animal" side that can be controlled by reason only *imperfectly*. So maybe, in a moment of intense emotion, you utter the wrong words. Later: "How could I have said such an unkind thing to her! What a jerk!" And let's not get into sexual indiscretions or other cases of weakness of will when you let strong physical desires cloud your judgment. Demanding moral perfection may therefore be a reasonable possibility if you happen to be a disembodied spirit inhabiting a perfect world (heaven), but here on earth, where you are a flesh-and-blood human animal, your moral judgment is going to be imperfect.

Moral Uncertainty and Ambiguity

Perhaps you are familiar with the line, "the best-laid plans of mice and men often go awry"—adapted from Robert Burns's "The best laid schemes o' mice an' men / Gang aft a-gley" (Burns, n.d.). In Burns's poem, the mouse sets up his home in the field with the intention of finding safety and food, only to face the farmer's plough and be chased away. No doubt, like the mouse, you have set your plans with the best of intentions and things have gone awry. Perhaps you tried your best to do only good for your children, your parents, or your friends, but things simply didn't go according to plan. Then: "Oh, I should have known better! Why didn't I see that coming? It's all my fault!" The difference between you and the mouse, says Burns, is that you look backward to the misfortune, lament it, and cast blame, and then look forward with uncertainty and fear, whereas the mouse sees only the present, and therefore suffers less in the end. But like the mouse, none of us can realistically demand that we never make a mistake in judgment, no matter how careful we may be!

Not only is it not always possible to predict moral outcomes, but the correct moral option may not even be clear. Suppose you can either help a friend study for an exam or spend the time reviewing for your own exam. Are you being a bad friend if you choose to review for your own exam? Are you being unfair to yourself if you choose to help your friend? And, to leap straight to one of the greatest social divides of our times, is it ever morally permissible to have an abortion?

Moral Conflicts

Situations can and do arise where two of your moral principles conflict, so that satisfying one of them violates another. For example, should you lie to a friend to avoid upsetting him? If you tell the truth, you risk upsetting him; if you lie, or omit the truth, you violate your principles of truth-telling and honesty. Either way, you appear to violate one of your moral principles.

The Absolutism of Demanding Moral Perfection

When you're a moral perfectionist, moral conflicts are likely to weigh heavily on your psyche, leaving you with an intense guilty aftertaste no matter what you do. This is unavoidable when you demand perfection in the way of moral decisions, because by their nature moral conflicts require accepting less than *perfect* solutions. For example, making a decision to sign a do not resuscitate (DNR) order for a beloved, very ill parent or grandparent in the event the patient goes into cardiac arrest can be daunting, even in cases where the quality of life and prognosis are extremely poor.

The Guilt of Moral Perfectionism

Being rational does *not* mean being insensitive or unfeeling. So you decide to disconnect Grandpa from life support. Such a decision can be both rational and intensely emotional. In contrast, the guilt generated by moral perfectionism is, almost invariably, unhealthy and debilitating: "I should have visited him more when I had the opportunity. I'm a terrible person!"

This does not mean that all guilt is unhealthy and debilitating. Some guilt can lead you to make constructive changes when the guilt focuses on the deed, not the doer. In contrast, the guilt generated by moral perfectionism:

- Involves damning the doer rather than the deed

- Leads to rumination

- Promotes depression

When the moral perfectionist falls short of satisfying her unrealistic perfectionistic demand, she tends to go for her own jugular: "What a horrible person I am. How could I have said those horrible things to him?" It is precisely this painful consciousness of being a *bad person* for having committed the perceived moral offense that defines the guilt. Such self-damning guilt can gnaw away at your self-respect and often leads to depression. You come to perceive yourself as undeserving of anything of value and therefore feel futile and hopeless about the prospects for a worthwhile existence. Here, being a "bad" or "horrible" person does not mean you are wicked or evil but is a more global moral condemnation of self. *It is a debasement of your respectability or deservingness as a person.* Being a bad person, in this sense, means that you are unworthy of being treated with the dignity and respect we accord morally decent human beings. While in such a disempowering state of mind, it is unlikely that you will take the initiative to engage in constructive, life-affirming activities. Instead, you will be more inclined to ruminate about just how bad you are, and to stew in your own self-degradation. This is moral purgatory!

"Well, maybe I deserve to suffer! So what's wrong with punishing myself?" The answer is that true repentance is constructive—and leads to welcome change. The self-damning guilt of moral perfectionism leads to the opposite result. Better to address your past actions, if they were misguided, and resolve to do things differently in the future! Exercise 6.1 gives you a chance to practice.

EXERCISE 6.1. Reflect on Your Moral Guilt

Think about a situation in which you experienced intense guilt about an action you think was wrong. In your journal, write down your responses to these questions:

- *What did you tell yourself about yourself? Were you self-critical? Explain.*

- *How much time did you spend thinking about this situation?*

- *What was your behavioral response? For instance, did you worry a lot? Did the guilt lead you to behave differently from your usual? If so, in what ways?*

- *Did you experience any other emotions besides guilt?*

- *Some moral perfectionists become defensive when they think another is suggesting they've done something morally wrong. In general, how do you respond when someone does this? Why do you think you respond in this way?*

The Anxiety of Moral Perfectionism

Moral perfectionists experience debilitating guilt and often depression over perceived *past* moral misjudgments. Even more, they also experience anxiety about the possibility of *future* misjudgments.

Generalized Moral Anxiety

Moral perfectionists tend to have generalized moral anxiety (GMA)— the fear of future moral misjudgments, generalized to diverse life situations:

- "What if I make a mistake and someone gets hurt?"

- "What if I let my kids down?"

- "What if I make a promise I'm unable to keep?"

- "What if I upset my mother by being honest with her?"

- "What if I do a lousy job when everyone is depending on me?"

Most moral perfectionists would respond: "I would be a *bad person!*" Sadly, such conjecture of possible future misjudgment and moral self-condemnation can pile up with other perceived past misdeeds, leading to guilt, depression, *and* anxiety.

The ever-present possibility of faltering in the future is a defining feature of GMA. The anxiety persists, while its objects tend to change. Today it's how to perfectly resolve a perceived moral dilemma at home; tomorrow, it's a problem at work.

Self-Critical Dilemma Thinking

Moral perfectionists also often face this dilemma: no matter what they do, the outcome will be morally imperfect, which will reflect negatively on them. Thus they experience intense anxiety: "I promised to take Johnny to Disney World today, and he's been so looking forward to it. But he still has a slight fever! If I take him, he might have a relapse. But I promised, and it'll break his little heart! Either way, I'll be a terrible mom! What should I do? I'm damned if I do and damned if I don't!"

Procrastination

In ruminating and worrying about the negative alternatives of a perceived moral dilemma, it is easy to lose your bearings and *procrastinate*, not knowing whether, when, or what to do to avoid doing something less than perfectly moral. You may end up making your decision *by indecision*—doing nothing to reasonably address your situation. For example, because you don't want to hurt your boyfriend by ending the relationship, you say nothing and continue to date someone you don't really love.

EXERCISE 6.2. Reflect on Your Other Behavioral and Emotional Responses

Reflect on the following prompt and questions, and write your answers in your journal.

1. Imagine a possible situation in which you do something you think would be less than morally perfect that you think would reflect negatively on you as a person, and that creates considerable anxiety just to contemplate. Example: "What if I *do something to lose my job when I am the only source of income for my family*?" (You will refer back to this example later.)

2. Do you ever perceive challenging situations in your everyday life as self-critical moral dilemmas? If so, provide an example.

3. Do you ever procrastinate because you think your alternatives are all less than morally perfect? If so, provide an example, and explain how you finally dealt with this situation.

4. Do you ever end up making your decisions by indecision because your alternatives are all less than morally ideal? If so, provide an example.

Keeping your responses to Exercises 6.1 and 6.2 in mind, let's now address your moral perfectionism by applying the six-step method.

Step 1: Identify Your Irrational Thinking

Consider the reasoning that drives the *guilt* of moral perfectionism:

1. I must be perfectly moral.

2. Therefore, if I fall short of being perfectly moral, then I'm a bad person.

3. I have fallen short of being perfectly moral.

4. Therefore, I'm a bad person.

With this irrational logic, you set yourself up as unworthy of respect— a bleak outlook that can take a toll on your emotional health. With Exercise 6.3, you'll explore your own version of this irrational logic.

EXERCISE 6.3. Identify Your Guilty Reasoning

1. Consider again the situation you discussed in Exercise 6.1 in which you experienced intense guilt about something you think you did that was wrong. Try to sum it up in as few words as possible (for example, "lied to my best friend," or "deliberately said something I knew would upset her").

2. Now copy the following reasoning template in your journal, inserting your brief descriptions:

   1. I must be perfectly moral.

   2. Therefore, if I [*brief description*], then I am a bad person.

   3. I [*brief description*].

   4. Therefore, I am a bad person.

This is it: the actual reasoning you use to make yourself feel guilty! You can use this template to expose other instances of your guilty reasoning.

The Reasoning That Drives Your Anxiety

As you have seen, guilt and depression are not the only emotional tolls that moral perfectionism can exact. Anxiety, particularly generalized moral anxiety reasoning (GMA), is another emotional price you pay for being a moral perfectionist.

The basic reasoning undergirding GMA goes like this:

1. I must be perfectly moral.

2. Therefore, *if* I (ever) fall short of being perfectly moral, I'll be a bad person.

From the demand for moral perfection in premise 1 you deduce the *possibility* of becoming a bad person *if* you fall short of moral perfection. It is this uncertain or "iffy" character of your conclusion in premise 2 that hangs over you and makes you anxious. So any possible situation in which you think you might fall short of moral perfection will make you anxious! Exercise 6.4 will help you identify the particular premises behind some of your own GMA reasoning.

EXERCISE 6.4. Identify Your Generalized Moral Anxiety Reasoning

1. In Exercise 6.2, question 1, you provided an example of a possible situation in which you did something wrong. Summarize it briefly.

2. Now copy the following reasoning template in your journal, inserting your brief description:

    1. I must be perfectly moral.

    2. Therefore, *if* I fall short of being perfectly moral, then I'll be a bad person.

    3. If I [*brief description*], then I'll fall short of being perfectly moral.

    4. Therefore, if I [*brief description*], I'll be a bad person.

You have just identified the actual reasoning you use to make yourself anxious about this possibility! Now that you have the template, use it to expose other instances of GMA reasoning that generate much needless anxiety for you.

Step 2: Refute Your Irrational Premises

Here is where you show your demand for moral perfection and your self-damnation to be irrational.

Refute Your Demand for Moral Perfection

By now, it should be clear that the root of your self-defeating guilt and anxiety is none other than the premise that says you *must* be perfectly moral. If ever there were a setup for defeat, this is it! You simply can't be perfectly moral for the reasons already stated: moral standards often conflict; you are not omniscient and therefore cannot predict moral outcomes with anywhere near 100 percent accuracy; what's morally right or wrong can be ambiguous and subject to interpretation; moral standards are not absolute; and last but not least, you are an imperfect human being and therefore subject to misjudgment.

Refute Your Self-Damnation

So can you honestly say that being morally imperfect makes you morally disrespectable or undeserving as a person? This would mean not just you, but each and every other imperfect human being, past, present, and future, is also morally unfit. You'd be saying that Albert Schweitzer and Mother Teresa are likewise moral misfits. Both are often-cited pillars of morality: the former taught reverence for life, while the latter dedicated her life to helping the poor, sick, and underserved. Yet they also were not morally perfect (Hines, 2018; Wagner, n.d.). To be consistent, you'll need to give up your self-damning inference when you too prove to be less than morally perfect.

Step 3: Identify Your Guiding Virtues

Now it's time to identify some constructive thinking! On your journey toward greater self-security in a world where no human being can be morally perfect, here are three goals for making peace with imperfection.

Unconditional Self-Acceptance

Moral perfectionists base their self-respect on whether their lives conform to their absolutistic ideal of morality, leading to a lifetime roller-coaster ride of guilt, depression, and anxiety. You can overcome this self-destructive view of your moral self by cultivating a habit of *unconditional* self-acceptance.

Courage

To overcome your anxiety, you will need to cultivate the courage to:

- Accept the uncertain, ambiguous nature of what's morally right and wrong

- Make moral decisions and act on them in the face of your inherent moral fallibility

Prudence

Excessive worry and rumination does not help you rationally resolve moral challenges; rather, it creates self-sabotaging stress. Prudence reinforces your ability to tolerate the uncertainty and ambiguity of moral decisions by cultivating constructive, creative ways to approach moral challenges instead of casting moral choices as hopeless dilemmas or unrealistic ideals.

Step 4: Gain Philosophical Wisdom from the Sages

To develop unconditional self-acceptance, Thomas Jefferson said to embrace your "unalienable rights to life, liberty, and the pursuit of happiness." It would be odd (and self-defeating) if these famous Jeffersonian words in the United States Declaration of Independence (1776) were taken to apply to the government's respect for its citizens but not to the citizens' respect for themselves. The word "unalienable" is especially important here. It means that *you don't have to be perfect* to enjoy these fundamental human rights.

Immanuel Kant said you don't have to be morally perfect to deserve respect (*Internet Encyclopedia of Philosophy*, n.d.). This great champion of unconditional self-worth recognized that no one on earth could be morally perfect. You'll never be perfect, so stop *damning yourself when you're not*. Like your rights to life, liberty, and the pursuit of happiness, your self-worth is unalienable. So you can admit that you *did something* dumb, but that doesn't make *you* dumb!

To develop courage, Jean-Paul Sartre said to be proactive, not passive (Sartre, 1989). According to Sartre, you will never find absolute proof that your choice is the right one. In the face of this inherent uncertainty and ambiguity, the act of choosing, in itself, makes your choice the right one. The courageous person doesn't make any excuses and accepts responsibility for what he decides to do.

To develop prudence, Aristotle said, don't confuse morals with math (Aristotle, 1941, bk. 1, ch. 3). This great sage tells you to avoid going to extremes—and demanding that you have the same level of certainty and precision in moral decision-making as you have in mathematics is an extreme. The prudent person realizes that it is *reasonable* belief, not certainty, that matters: "I don't know for sure that putting my child in day care is right, but it will be good for Timmy's social development, and it will give me a respite."

Step 5: Build a Rational Plan of Action

What do you do now to disturb yourself when you confront making a moral decision? Moral perfectionists often:

- Procrastinate about making and/or acting on a decision

- Make decisions by indecision

- Create a self-critical moral dilemma and ruminate about it

- Tell themselves that they'd be a bad person if they didn't worry about what to do

- Distract themselves with something else so they don't have to confront making the decision

- Try to get someone else to make the decision for them

What do *you* do to disturb yourself when you think a moral decision you've *already* made is morally imperfect? Here are some possibilities:

- Become defensive when someone else suggests you might have done something even remotely morally wrong

- Wallow in self-blame and damnation

- Ruminate, going over and over what you coulda, shoulda done

- Withdraw from or avoid social encounters

- Refrain from constructive activities or things you like to do

- Act unfriendly or disagreeable toward others

- Have a difficult time concentrating or focusing on other things

EXERCISE 6.5. How Do You Approach Moral Decision-Making?

Reflect on the following two questions and jot down your responses in your journal.

1. Think about the last moral decision you had to make that created significant stress. What did you do to disturb yourself about making and acting on a decision? For example, did you perceive it as a self-critical moral dilemma and wallow in it? Make a list of whatever you recall that you did to disturb yourself.

2. Recall the situation you described in Exercise 6.1 in which you experienced guilt about a perceived wrongdoing. List whatever you recall that you did to sustain your guilt. For example, did you continue to blame yourself and tell yourself what a bad person you are?

What Would the Sages Tell You to Do Differently?

Here's some pointed advice our sages would give you:

- Kant: Stop damning yourself when you inevitably prove to be morally imperfect.

- Jefferson: Assert your "declaration of independence" from self-tyranny by refusing to be constrained by self-destructive worrying; instead, seek out meaningful, pleasant encounters with others.

- Sartre: Stop procrastinating, creating unsolvable dilemmas, or otherwise trying to hide your freedom and responsibility. Don't look for absolutes. Make it right by choosing!

- Aristotle: Don't go to extremes. It's moral ambiguity, not math. Choose and act on what you think is reasonable, not perfect.

EXERCISE 6.6. Create Your Plan of Action

1. Identify your behavioral responses. In Exercise 6.5, you created two lists of the things you did to disturb yourself when you faced making a moral decision or had made one you thought was wrong. What would each of our great thinkers tell you to do differently?

2. Create your plan of action. Based on these insights, make another creative to-do list of those things. *This new list will be your plan of action!*

Step 6: Put Your Plan of Action into Practice

You are now ready to start working toward your guiding virtues: unconditional self-acceptance, courage, and prudence! You'll be putting your best foot forward to apply the wisdom of the sages. Chapter Fourteen will help you continue building your new skills in making peace with being morally imperfect. As you work through that chapter, keep these three key ideas in mind:

- In demanding moral perfection, you are demanding more of yourself than even the most famous pillars of morality in history were capable of achieving.

- Your respectability and deservingness as a human being do not depend on your being perfect—not even near-perfect.

- Moral decision-making is inherently uncertain and ambiguous. There's simply no mathematical formula for always doing the morally right thing.

If you have other types of imperfection to make peace with, feel free to continue with the other type-specific chapters—but be sure you've first worked through Exercises 14.1 and 14.2, so you are familiar with the final step of the method.

CHAPTER 7

Control Perfectionism

Control perfectionists try to control other people's actions or circumstances. In fact, they place a *demand* on themselves that they achieve such control. They are trying to prevent bad things from happening to:

- The people whose actions or circumstances they try to control ("I must prevent you from doing something stupid that you'll regret!")

- Other people they care about ("I must convince my son's teacher to give him an A so it won't ruin his average")

- Themselves ("I must not let others think they can take advantage of me")

Control perfectionists are not power brokers who seek to wield power or control for its own sake. They do not have an intrinsic interest in dominating others or controlling their lives; rather, they are generally well-meaning folks concerned with protecting others or themselves from harm. Unfortunately, control perfectionism tends to create considerable emotional stress for the control perfectionist as well as others with whom they live or work.

Common emotional responses exhibited by control perfectionists are:

- Anxiety about the possibility of not being able to control the actions or circumstances of others

- Guilt about not doing or having done enough to successfully exercise such control

- Depression arising from self-blame due to such perceived failure to control outcomes

- Anger or deep resentment toward others whose actions they have been unable to control

Now, let's look at the profiles of some typical control perfectionists.

Smothering Mothering

This married, fifty-two-year-old mother of two adult children loved her children deeply, and the thought of anything bad happening to them often filled her with dread. Driven by intense, persistent fear, she attempted to head off any potential dangers she perceived might befall them. She spent much of her life involving herself with their personal decisions. She called them up regularly for updates on their lives, and they called her frequently to ask her advice. The result was codependency: the children became overly dependent on their faithful mom, and Mom became much too involved in their private matters. "I don't think you should go out with that boy again. He comes from a divorced home. He's likely to divorce you too if you should get serious and marry him." The children resented her intrusive advice but nonetheless persisted in asking for it. It was not until this doting mom began to work on overcoming her demand to control her children that the family began to progress toward overcoming the codependency.

Never Having Done Enough

This gentleman worried constantly about whether he did enough to prevent harm to others. "I should have told John that romaine lettuce from Arizona was recalled when he ordered a salad with romaine lettuce in it. What if he ate that bad lettuce, and I could have prevented it?" Sadly, such thoughts would keep him up ruminating instead of sleeping: "I shouldn't have told Barbara that Jody was flirting with Bob at the office. What if she thinks he's having an affair and they end up getting a divorce because of me? I better fix this by telling her tomorrow that Bob was not interested in Jody. But what if she doesn't believe me?" What if this, and what if that? How to control all these "what ifs" preoccupied him and disrupted his sleep. This overwhelming perfectionistic demand to control the fate of others, and the inevitable failure to meet it, kept him in a needless, suspended, painful state of guilt.

Controlling What Others Might Think

"I must make sure others don't talk trash about me!" was the mantra of this young male business executive obsessed with controlling his image. He constantly tried to feed others information about himself that placed him in a positive light, and he was preoccupied with preventing them from finding out anything about him that might change their minds. For example, his former girlfriend had posted a photo of him on Facebook in which he was drunk, wearing a pair of women's bikini underwear on his head. "I was just kidding around when my former girlfriend took that pic," he said to a group of prospective clients, not knowing if any of them either saw or even cared about the photo. "I wasn't high or anything," he strategically added. Unfortunately, the more he attempted to control the opinions of others, the more turned off to him they became, and the more they talked trash about him!

Controlling the Audience's Response

This undergraduate music major and classical guitarist experienced strong anxiety whenever he played before large audiences, such as at university recitals, so he was willing to perform only relatively easy-to-execute compositions. Yet in the solitude of his apartment, with no one watching, he was astonishing at executing even the most difficult passages of Villa-Lobos, whose compositions challenged even the most accomplished classical guitarists. Unfortunately, this talented soul was more intent on controlling the response from his audience than on performing; consequently, despite his selection of relatively easy compositions, his public performances were not nearly as adept as when he played in solitude.

Maintaining a Tight Ship of Life

"I must be in control. Otherwise, bad things will happen." Married, with one twelve-year-old child, this woman always *had to be* on top of things, for fear her family members might not succeed. She enforced a rigorous schedule for her child, dictating when he had to do his homework and when he could hang out with his friends. She hovered over him like a helicopter to make sure that his homework was done "perfectly," and she was well known among her child's school faculty for attempting to control the quality of instruction her child received. She also micromanaged her husband; the poor man received his marching orders daily. "Don't forget to pay the electric bill today!" "Go to the grocery store after work and pick up a few groceries." "You need to remove that dead tree on Saturday." "You need to make a dentist's appointment this week to get that chipped tooth capped." The demands and commands kept coming in a steady stream. Although she meant well, the stress she created for all concerned overbalanced any positive value she might have provided.

How Do *You* Try to Control Others?

I know you are well meaning, like the folks in these examples, but owning up to your attempts to control others can save you from the abyss of much unnecessary stress. Exercise 7.1 can help!

EXERCISE 7.1. Over What Are You Demanding Control?

Think about the following questions and write down your responses in your journal.

1. Based on what you've read in this chapter so far, make a list of the things over which you demand control. For example, do you demand control over specific aspects of the lives of family, children, or friends? Do you try to control how others view you, and how audiences respond to you when you are speaking in public, making a presentation, or

giving a recital? Do you try to control virtually everything and everyone in your life, or at least those who are important to you?

2. What feelings do you experience when your demands for control are not satisfied? For example, guilt when you think you haven't done enough, anxiety that a loved one will make a serious mistake unless you control their actions, or depression?

3. Can you identify with any of the examples of control perfectionism provided in this chapter? Which ones and in what respect/s?

Keeping your responses to Exercise 7.1 in mind, apply the six-step method to your control perfectionism.

Step 1: Identify Your Irrational Thinking

Here's the general line of reasoning that propels control perfectionism:

1. I *must* prevent harm to myself or certain others whom I care about.

2. If I don't control these actions/circumstances, they or I will be harmed.

3. Therefore, I *must* control these actions/circumstances.

4. Therefore, if I don't control these actions/circumstances, it would be awful.

For instance, the smothering mother described earlier tells herself she must prevent any harm whatsoever to her adult children. She thinks that if she doesn't control their decisions, they will be harmed; therefore, she *must* control their decisions, and it would be awful if she doesn't.

See how this reasoning can create looming anxiety, with the possibility of not meeting your demand for control continuously hanging over your head? Worse, if you actually fall short of your demand for control, and the harm does happen, you may blame yourself, feel guilty about it, and even fall into a deep depression. This reasoning can really be a downer if you don't identify and kill it before it multiplies!

It's essential that you identify the premises of your own self-destructive thinking, refute them, and change your thinking to something much more constructive. Start by identifying your reasoning with Exercise 7.2.

EXERCISE 7.2. Identify Your Reasoning

Complete the following, recording the results in your journal.

1. In Exercise 7.1, you listed the things over which you demand control. Choose one over which you tend to demand the most control or that most concerns you. Then briefly describe it: "My child's homework"; "My employees' job performance"; "What others think of me"; "What happens to other people I know."

2. In this reasoning template, enter the brief description and the individual/s you want to protect:

    1. I must prevent harm to [*individual/s to be protected*].

    2. If I don't control [*action/s or circumstance/s*], then [*individual/s*] will be harmed.

    3. Therefore, I must control [*action/s or circumstance/s*].

    4. Therefore, if I don't control [*action/s or circumstance/s*], it would be awful.

Congratulations! Your completed template is the reasoning you have used to upset yourself when you demand control.

Step 2: Refute Your Irrational Premises

Now look carefully at your premises, with an eye to debunking them.

Refute Your *Musts*

You are telling yourself that you *must* protect those you care about, so you further think you *must* control certain actions or circumstances that could harm them. So you have two *musts*, one deduced from the other:

1. I must prevent harm to this person.

2. Therefore, I must control the person's actions or circumstances leading to any such harm.

However, both *musts* are false, because there is simply no lawful necessity or "must" by which you can perfectly control such external events. The human capacity to control the external world is limited and imperfect. Accepting this cognitively and emotionally is the key to overcoming your control perfectionism!

Refute Your Awfulizing

You are also making this unsound inference:

1. I *must* control the actions or circumstances leading to the harm in question.

2. Therefore, if I don't control these actions or circumstances, it would be awful.

This inference is unsound because, again, the "must" from which it proceeds is not factual. A helicopter mom might refute this inference by telling herself, "Yes, it's *unfortunate* if I can't always control how others treat my child or the situations she gets into, but that doesn't make it *awful*." She can take reasonable precautions to protect her child. For example, she can teach her child not to trust strangers. But she can't guarantee that things will always happen as she wishes.

Step 3: Identify Your Guiding Virtues

It's time to set goals that can help you attain greater security in a world that is not always under your control. Such guiding virtues include *courage*, self-control in the exercise of *tolerance*, and *prudence*.

Courage

For overcoming control perfectionism, exercising courage means to stand firmly against your tendency to overreact to and exaggerate how much control you have over possible harm to others or to yourself. At one extreme, some people shy away from dangers they can and probably should try to control. At the other extreme, the control perfectionist overzealously demands control over what is not in her control, and consequently generates needless stress. The courageous person avoids both extremes and therefore does not demand perfect control.

Tolerance

Here, this guiding virtue involves allowing others to exercise their own autonomy and discretion instead of trying to control them, even if you mean it for their own good or the good of others.

Prudence

In this context, prudence involves knowing your own limits of control and how to work within them to effect positive change, including avoiding harm to others or to yourself.

Step 4: Gain Philosophical Wisdom from the Sages

The attainment of each of these guiding virtues has been the subject of much philosophical reflection in the history of ideas. So what wisdom of the sages can be gleaned to help you attain them?

To exercise courage, Epictetus admonishes against trying to control what is not ours to control. His philosophy of control can be summed up as follows:

- You can only fully control *your own* actions and responses.

- You cannot fully control other people's actions, or the conditions under which they act. Other people have their own minds, and what you think *should or must* be often does not happen.

- Thus when you try to control other people's actions, or the conditions under which they act, you set yourself up for lamentation, perturbation, fault-finding, feeling hindered, and many other forms of discontent.

- On the other hand, if you stick to what is completely in your control—namely, your own actions—you will avoid these negative consequences and instead enjoy peace of mind (Epictetus, 1948).

Control perfectionists unrealistically attempt to control other people's actions or the conditions under which they act, creating needless stress.

So courage means realizing your limitations in controlling others and sticking to what is yours to control: your own actions. The helicopter mom exercises courage when she lets go of trying to control how others treat her child and also gives him some age-appropriate autonomy (say, doing his own homework); the classical guitarist exercises courage when he focuses on his performance and not on what his audience thinks of it; and the young business executive exercises courage when he stops trying to control whether others are talking trash about him.

To exercise tolerance, Immanuel Kant tells us to respect others as rationally self-determining persons. As discussed in Chapter Three, Kant distinguishes between objects and persons; the latter can make their own decisions (Kant, 1964). So Kant entreats us to exercise tolerance for others by treating them as persons and not mere objects. This means letting them decide and act for themselves.

Abraham Lincoln addressed the need *to exercise prudence* in our attempts to control others, stating: "No man is good enough to govern another man without the other's consent." Lincoln, speaking specifically of slavery, continued, "The master not only governs the slave without his consent; but he governs him by a set of rules altogether different from those which he prescribes for himself" (Lincoln, 1854). Lincoln's prudence is edifying! You wouldn't want to be governed without your consent, so don't do the same to others.

Lincoln and Kant concur: treat human beings not like property, but as rational, self-determining persons.

Psychologist Carl Rogers tells us to *be facilitators rather than directors*. Whereas the former promotes autonomy, the latter stifles it: "You will give me a heart attack if you don't listen to me!" said that smothering mother, trying to dissuade her daughter from dating the son of divorced parents. Some control perfectionists think the end always justifies the means, but this is imprudent, because it leads to dysfunction and tends to be self-defeating. You seek to protect someone from harm but instead create hard feelings. "It's your fault I turned down that guy. I should never have listened to you! Now I'm alone, and have no one!"

In contrast, Carl Rogers (2012) would advise the mother to facilitate rather than direct change; to ask open-ended questions ("How do you feel about this new guy?") and to reflect back the daughter's responses in a manner that helps clarify her feelings. "So it sounds like you're really attracted to him, but you have some anxiety about seeing him again. Would you like to talk about it?" Here, the goal is the daughter's autonomous decision, one less likely to end in finger pointing and resentment.

Step 5: Build a Rational Plan of Action

With some pertinent wisdom of the sages under your belt, let's look into building a plan of action whereby you can apply it to your guiding virtues. What are you doing now that you could do differently based on your new insights?

In situations in which control perfectionists demand control, they often:

- Focus on controlling others rather than on what *they* are doing

- Are insensitive to others' feelings ("Just suck it up!")

- Attempt to intimidate others into listening to them ("You would be foolish to go out with him")

- Threaten or bully others ("I'll remember this next time you want something from me")

- Ruminate about whether they have done enough ("What if she gets sick and it's my fault?")

- Refuse to compromise with those with whom they disagree ("You just need to listen to me")

- Withdraw from social contact ("I feel so powerless")

- Blame themselves for not controlling others' actions or decisions ("It's my fault; I should have insisted!")

- Appeal to pity ("I'm gonna have a heart attack if you do that!")

What are *your* behavioral responses? Exercise 7.3 can help with this question.

EXERCISE 7.3. What Are Your Behavioral Responses?

Recall your choice in Exercise 7.2, item 1—something about which you especially demand control—and respond to these questions in your journal:

1. Have you exhibited any of the behavioral responses just listed? If so, which ones, and in what ways?

2. What are your behavioral responses when your demand is not satisfied? List as many as you can think of.

What Would the Sages Tell You to Do Differently?

Fortunately, you now have some new insights that you can use to redirect your behavioral responses toward your guiding virtues. So here's some pertinent advice from our sages.

EPICTETUS

- Focus on your own actions, not on what others are doing or thinking. Only the former is yours to control!

- Stop ruminating about not controlling the actions of others, or blaming yourself for this "failure."

- Enjoy social contact with others—*this* is in your power.

KANT

Instead of attempting to intimidate others—to bully or threaten them, appeal to pity, or try to force your ways on them—treat them as people, not objects to be controlled. Allow them to exercise their own rational self-determination on matters concerning themselves. Each of us has our own rational capacities, which are *ours* to control.

LINCOLN

- Get others' consent before trying to tell them what to do.

- Threatening, intimidating, bullying, manipulating by trying to evoke pity, and other means of imposing your will on others is a poor strategy for getting what you want. Be practical: would you want to cooperate with others if they treated you like that?

- Be flexible and open to others' ideas.

CARL ROGERS

- Instead of telling people what to do, facilitate open-ended discussion. People will be more willing to engage with you and possibly come to reasonable decisions.

- Be open to exploring others' ideas instead of setting yourself up as the director.

- Be willing to explore other people's feelings through open-ended questions and reflection.

Are you ready to reflect on what *you would* do differently? Working through Exercise 7.4 can help!

EXERCISE 7.4. Create Your Plan of Action

In Exercise 7.2 you selected something about which you especially demand control. In Exercise 7.3, you listed the ways you respond, behaviorally, when you demand control.

1. Identify your behavioral responses. Now think about what our sages have advised and what each might tell you to do differently in the case you selected. For example, what would Epictetus tell you to do differently if you become focused on your audience instead of your speech?

2. Create your plan of action. Based on these insights, brainstorm another creative list of the things you would do differently. *This new list will be your plan of action!*

Step 6: Put Your Plan of Action into Practice

Now it's time to apply what you've learned in this chapter by working toward your guiding virtues—courage, tolerance, and prudence. Launch the plan of action you developed in Exercise 7.4, keeping these three key ideas in mind:

- The human capacity to control the external world, in particular other people's actions or the conditions under which they act, is limited and imperfect.

- Focusing on controlling *your* actions, not the actions of others, tends to bring peace of mind.

- It's not awful to not be perfectly in control!

Congratulations on working through this chapter! To implement your plan of action for making peace with your limits of control over the external world, proceed to Chapter Fourteen. Feel free to continue with the other type-specific chapters—but first work through Exercises 14.1 and 14.2, so you can begin to make constructive changes.

CHAPTER 8

Expectation Perfectionism

Expectation perfectionists demand perfection, or near-perfection, of others in general or certain others with whom they have a relationship, imposing rigid, perfectionistic standards on their children, employees, teachers, students, friends, significant others, service providers, and more. When they think these standards have not been, or may not be, satisfied, their emotional responses tend to be exaggerated, and may include:

- Anxiety

- Depression

- Sadness

- Anger, including rage

- Shock (as distinct from disappointment or surprise)

The expectations of these perfectionists tend to be:

- Unrealistic (impossible or extremely difficult to satisfy)

- Unconditional (without or almost without exception)

- Grandiose (overly ambitious)

- Burdensome (overly imposing on others)

- Demanding (others must be perfect or near-perfect)

EXERCISE 8.1. Reflect on Your Behavioral and Emotional Responses

How do you respond emotionally when others do not live up to your performance expectations for them? In your journal, jot down your most common responses.

There are a number of common manifestations of expectation perfectionism. Expectation perfectionists may demand that:

- Their children always get straight A's, or 100 percent on exams

- Significant others always meet their domestic responsibilities perfectly (for example, always having dinner ready on time or cleaning the house without missing a speck)

- Service providers provide perfect service (for example, eliminating any waiting)

- Employees never mess up or be late or absent from work

- Teachers never make a grading error

- Friends make heroic sacrifices for them

- Others always obey social niceties (for example, never cut in line, always hold the door for you)

Let's look more closely at some of these examples.

The Overzealous Parent

I know of many parents who expect their children to perform perfectly or near-perfectly in school, sports, or other activities. One mom became a regular at her daughter's school, leveling complaints about teachers for unfairly grading her daughter. They were "terrible teachers," she proclaimed, and were "singling out" her daughter; that's why her little A-student was getting B's! As mother grilled and drilled daughter in preparation for upcoming exams and made sure all assignments and homework were impeccably accurate and in good form, both experienced intense, relentless anxiety. What a way to live!

The Hyperbolic Professor

I knew this tortured soul personally. An economics professor with some very credible publications, he was not very well liked among students, because most couldn't satisfy his grandiose requirements, so only 40 percent passed his courses. "This is the university, and my students need to toe the line!" he was fond of saying. Even one typo cost students a letter grade. He poured over student papers, looking for every conceivable type of grammatical error, not to mention trivial content inaccuracies. No typos allowed! Students were expected to have perfect attendance, and, you guessed it, "No excused absences!" A student who missed even one session lost another letter grade. And if a student missed an exam, that's right: no make-ups. The student received a zero! Unfortunately, this brilliant professor is no longer teaching, because he was given an early retirement.

The Slave-Driving Manager

A manager of a department store expected his sales crew to be busy at all times. No one could sit down even for a moment. If the shelves were neat and tidy, he would ask personnel to mess them up and then redo them so that they looked busy at all times. If an employee was ever idle, the irate manager berated her: "You are not being paid to stare out into space! Get back to work *now!*" Not surprisingly, this store had an extremely high employee turnover rate.

The Overly Demanding Customer

To give you an idea of what I mean by "overly demanding," here's a dialog between the customer and a baker at a local bakery:

"What can I do for you, sir?"

"I bought this cake here and want my money back."

"I'm sorry about that, sir. What's wrong with it?"

"It's vanilla! It had chocolate icing, so I thought it was chocolate cake! No one told me it wasn't chocolate!"

"I'm so sorry. Would you like to exchange it for chocolate? We just finished decorating one. "

"No, I want a refund."

"Do you have the receipt?"

"No, just give me the damn refund!"

"I'm sorry, sir; without the receipt, I can give you store credit. Would you like that?"

"I'd like to throw this cake in your face, that's what I'd really like to do! Get your supervisor's butt out here—*now*!"

This particular customer believed the bakery made a mistake by not mentioning the cake was vanilla, so it *must* give him a refund without a receipt, even if this violated store policy. Such an expectation was grandiose, inflexible, and unrealistic. Unfortunately, it typified virtually all of this person's other interpersonal relationships.

EXERCISE 8.2. What Are Your Perfectionistic Expectations?

Think about the following questions and record your responses in your journal.

1. Based on what you've read in this chapter, list some perfectionistic expectations that you have of others.

2. When your expectations of someone are not satisfied, do you sometimes negatively rate *the person* as well as *the person's performance*? "What a stupid idiot! How could he have made such a dumb mistake!" Or do you usually negatively rate only the performance: "What you *did* was dumb!"?

3. Can you identify with any of the examples of expectation perfectionism provided in this chapter? If so, which ones, and in what respect/s?

Keeping your responses to Exercise 8.2 in mind, let's turn to our six-step method to begin working through your perfectionistic expectations!

Step 1: Identify Your Irrational Thinking

Take a good look at the basic reasoning that drives expectation perfectionism:

1. Others must perform perfectly/near-perfectly.

2. You didn't perform perfectly/near-perfectly.

3. Therefore, you are unworthy.

4. Therefore, I can't help being disturbed by you.

Notice how, from the perfectionistic demand in premise 1 and your not performing perfectly (or near-perfectly) in premise 2, you conclude in premise 3 that you or your performance is unworthy. Some expectation perfectionists, however, tend to negatively rate only the person's *performance*, but not *the person*. In either case, your imperfect performance means the perfectionist can't help being disturbed. Effectively, it's a zero tolerance policy!

Exercise 8.3 will help you key in to your own reasoning.

EXERCISE 8.3. Identify Your Reasoning

Do each of the following activities and write down the results in your journal:

1. In Exercise 8.2, question 1, you listed some of your own perfectionistic expectations of others. Select one and express it briefly: for example, "Get A's on all exams" or "Never miss a day of work."

2. Exercise 8.2, question 2 asked whether you sometimes negatively rate the person as well as the performance of a person who does not live up to your perfectionistic expectations. Regarding the expectation

you just selected, did you negatively rate only the deed, or also the person?

3. Now complete this reasoning template, using the expectation from question 1. For the subject you are negatively rating, if it's the *person*, enter "you"; otherwise, enter "your performance."

   1. You must [*perfectionistic expectation*].

   2. You didn't perform in this way.

   3. Therefore, [*the negatively rated subject*] is/are unworthy.

   4. Therefore, I can't help being disturbed by [*the negatively rated subject*].

Congratulations! Your filled-in template is the reasoning you use to upset yourself when the person in question has not satisfied your perfectionistic expectation.

Step 2: Refute Your Irrational Premises

Now that you've formulated your premises, you are in a position to carefully inspect them to see just why they are so destructive.

Refute Your *Must*

Premise 1 is the root of the problem. It is plainly false that mortal humans can satisfy your demand. So, you've set yourself up for an emotional tailspin as soon as you've embraced it. Also, how will others you place under such pressure feel? Ask the baker in the case of the customer from hell!

Refute Your Catastrophic Thinking

So you're catastrophizing about your child's getting a B (or about some other imperfect performance). I know, you want your child to be perfect, or at least damn near it, but if imperfection were automatically catastrophic, we'd all be doomed, because life on earth is imperfect!

Refute Your Damnation of Others

Likewise, if a person's not living up to your perfectionistic standards meant that he sucked, then everyone, or almost everyone, would suck. And how about you? Do you live up to your own perfectionistic standards? Be honest!

Refute Your *Can'tstipation*

Is it also really true that you *can't* help getting disturbed when others don't live up to your perfectionistic standards? Can you think of anyone who did not satisfy your standards yet you *didn't* get upset? What about your parents, or someone else you admire? Did any of them ever perform imperfectly without upsetting you? I suspect so; and if so, you *can* help getting disturbed.

Step 3: Identify Your Guiding Virtues

Instead of these irrational ideas, here are three guiding virtues that can help you make peace with a world where all human beings are imperfect.

Unconditional Other Acceptance

The acceptance of others, *whether or not they live up to your perfectionistic standards*, can help you embrace their inherent, human imperfection. This can, in turn, help you avoid the self-destructive emotions associated with unrealistically demanding perfection of others.

Courage

It can be helpful to work on your courage to confront the inevitability of imperfect future outcomes. In giving up your demand for perfection in others, you embrace their human imperfection—and your own. This can take courage!

Temperance

This form of self-control involves cultivating *temperance*—the ability to avoid self-destructive emotions—when others don't live up to your perfectionistic standards, and to realize that it is *you* who disturbs yourself, not others.

Step 4: Gain Philosophical Wisdom

To develop unconditional other acceptance, Albert Ellis advises us not to globally damn others. The grandfather of cognitive-behavioral therapy says to accept others because, just like you, they are living, breathing human beings with unique features (some good and some bad). Although you can constructively criticize the ill-advised things they may sometimes do, you do not damn them globally (call them degrading names) (Ellis, 2001).

The sixteenth-century political philosopher Thomas Hobbes says to treat others with the same dignity with which you would want to be treated. Hobbes puts his own spin on the golden rule: "Do not that to another which you would not have done to yourself" (Hobbes, 1939, 172). In disrespecting others by damning them, you endanger your own peace and security because they are likely to do the same—or worse—back. Albert Ellis agrees: "You do not want to be condemned, damned, or ostracized by people, therefore you unconditionally accept them" (Ellis, 2001, 30).

To develop courage, Buddha says, let go of your expectations about others. According to Buddhism, suffering stems from clinging to what is not in your control—and clearly the performance of others is one such thing. Courage here prescribes letting go of your perfectionistic expectations of others and letting things happen *as they do,* not as you think they *must* (Hanh, 2011).

To develop temperance, Epictetus says to own your emotions—do not speak as though life events are upsetting you when what's really upsetting you is the language you're using to refer to these events (Epictetus, 1948). Instead of saying, "You're an incompetent jerk!" try, "Too bad you're not doing as well as I hoped you'd do." And instead of saying, "Your incompetence is causing me nothing but grief!" fess up to the fact that you're causing your own grief!

Sartre says, to stop deceiving yourself and be authentic, ponder that "the man who hides behind his passions is deceiving himself," because "man is responsible for his passions" (Sartre, 1989). So you are simply lying to yourself when you tell yourself that others, not you, are pissing you off. The best proof that you can control your emotions is to simply do it: stop deceiving yourself, and be authentic. If you are lying to yourself, chances are you are not being honest with others, either. Sartre would say if you have something constructive to say, stop playing games and say it, then move on: "I think you could have landed that potential client if you spoke less and listened more attentively to what the client wanted to achieve in signing on with us."

Step 5: Build a Rational Plan of Action

When others do not live up to expectation perfectionist's demands, here are some common responses:

- Yelling or screaming at the person who has fallen short of their expectations

- Personally attacking the person (calling the person nasty names)

- Refusing to speak to the person

- Crying

- Being passive-aggressive (for example, the cold shoulder, nuanced digs or put-downs, and negative body language)

- Being physically aggressive

- Exacting retribution

Exercise 8.4 will help you identify your own behavioral responses.

EXERCISE 8.4. What Are Your Behavioral Responses?

In your journal, list as many things as you can think of that you do when others do not live up to your perfectionistic standards.

Now that you've absorbed the wisdom of the sages and identified your self-defeating behaviors, it's time to craft your very own plan of action with Exercise 8.5!

EXERCISE 8.5. Create Your Plan of Action

1. Identify your behavioral responses. In Exercise 8.4, you listed as many things you could think of that you presently do when others do not live up to your perfectionistic standards. Now, think of the sages' advice and what each might tell you to do differently. Suppose you act passive-aggressively with others when they make mistakes that you think are stupid. You've learned that you can exercise your willpower to stop delivering sarcastic remarks or put-downs and instead say something constructive and move on.

2. Create your plan of action. Based on these insights, make a creative list of the things you would do differently. *This new list will be your plan of action!*

Step 6: Put Your Plan of Action into Practice

As you work toward implementing the plan of action you created in Exercise 8.5, keep the following three ideas in mind:

- If people had to live up to your perfectionistic standards to be worthy of respect, then even the people you admire most, not to mention yourself, would rarely, if ever, be worthy of respect.

- Upsetting yourself over others' "imperfect" performances creates stress for yourself and others without serving any useful purpose.

- Your emotions don't just happen to you, like bolts of lightning striking you. You tend to have considerable control over them.

Congratulations for putting in a serious effort to work through the exercises in this chapter. To implement your plan of action for making peace with the imperfections of others, proceed to Chapter Fourteen. Feel free to continue with the other type-specific chapters—but be sure you've first worked through Exercises 14.1 and 14.2.

CHAPTER 9

Ego-Centered Perfectionism

Most of us prefer socializing and working with people who share at least some of our beliefs and values, especially outlooks we think are important, such as our religious or moral values. However, ego-centered perfectionism is not merely a preference; rather, it's a perfectionistic demand that other people always, or almost always, agree with your points of view, such as your beliefs, values, desires, interests, preferences, or tastes (Cohen, 2015).

Ego-centered perfectionists may:

- Get disturbed when other people disagree with them, sometimes even about small things

- Express unwillingness to see things from the perspectives of others who don't share their views

- Think that the viewpoints of others who disagree with them are not credible

- Think that others who don't agree with them are stupid, bad, or otherwise not worthy of their company

- Think that they always, or almost always, *have* to be right

- Rarely if ever admit that they are wrong

Your Subjective View Is Not the Only One!

We each see the world through our own subjective lens. This subjectivity is shaped by our personal, social, and cultural experiences. Our language, religious indoctrination, demographics, and other social, ethnic, gender, and cultural aspects coalesce with our personal experiences to form a complex belief system through which we interpret the world. So it's understandable that you would be more comfortable with your views of the world than with others' contrasting ones. Unfortunately, ego-centered perfectionists tend to view others' subjective views as false, misguided, misinformed, or otherwise defective, and to accord objective status to their own views, expressed emphatically, as in these examples:

- How can anyone like cats better than dogs?

- You must be insane to like snow!

- Only an idiot would vote for that candidate.

- Atheists are all heathens.

- Gay people are sick.

- Italian food is the best!

- My family (unlike yours) is a *real* family!

- I don't believe in that feminist crap, so get it out of your mind!

The common thread is that somehow your perspectives set the standard for what's real, true, good, healthy, and so forth. This suggests a very curious view of truth or reality that undergirds ego-centered perfectionism.

I doubt that you have ever explicitly said, "I set the standard of truth. I am the reality guru!" Nevertheless, for most ego-centered perfectionists, this view is implicit in the way they process others' views when they conflict with their own. Check this out for yourself by working through Exercise 9.1.

EXERCISE 9.1. Reflect on Your Own Ego-Centricity

In your journal, generate a list, similar to the preceding example, of your thoughts or statements that reveal your tendency to set the standard of truth or reality.

The Ego-Centered Perfectionist's Topsy-Turvy Theory of Truth

The essential definition of truth was long ago summed up by Aristotle: A belief is true when it corresponds to fact, and false when it doesn't (Aristotle, 1941, bk 4, pt. 7). So your belief that the earth revolves around the sun is true because there is such a fact, whereas the belief held by the churchmen of the Middle Ages that the sun revolves around the earth is false because there never was such a fact. In contrast, ego-centered perfectionists think that facts exist when they correspond to their perspectives (beliefs, values, desires, tastes, or preferences) and false when they don't. *The world revolves around them!*

Now, there are degrees to which someone might hold this topsy-turvy theory of truth. In the extreme, there are persons with narcissistic personality disorder, whose level of grandiosity and sense of self-importance is delusional (Cohen, 2017). Fortunately, most ego-centered perfectionists don't suffer from delusions of grandeur. Nevertheless, any tendency to perceive that your beliefs, values, preferences, desires, interests, and tastes are more valid than anyone else's can cause you a lot of personal and interpersonal strife.

Inability to Forge Successful Intimate Relationships

Ego-centered perfectionists generally have difficulty establishing and keeping satisfying intimate relationships because they stifle their partners' autonomy and self-expression. They don't recognize others' beliefs, values, preferences, tastes, and desires as valid if they differ from their own. Consequently, partners are driven to either give up their individuality or suffer persistent attempts to undermine, belittle, or otherwise degrade their status as distinct, autonomous persons. In either case, the relationship is dysfunctional and often short-lived.

Problems at Work

Ego-centered perfectionists do not generally fare well in the workplace for similar reasons. Insofar as they clash with colleagues, a constant state of antagonism arises, which generally ends with a pink slip. If the ego-centered perfectionist is in a managerial position, there is animosity and resentment among employees, which tends to impact employee productivity. As Daniel Goleman (1997) has shown, emotional intelligence, which includes other-regarding skills such as the ability to empathize with others, may be an even greater indicator of success in management than cognitive ability.

Inability to Learn and Adapt

Because they hate to admit mistakes, ego-centered perfectionists have a hard time learning and adapting to new situations. If you think you're always right, you are not going to make changes to correct what you have done wrong. You will be inflexible and impervious to change— setting yourself up for mismanaging your own life and the lives of others who may depend on you.

Stifling of Creativity

Because ego-centered perfectionists tend to dismiss other people's suggestions when they do not agree with their own ideas, they narrow the range of creative ideas from which they can draw in addressing life challenges. As most creative people will affirm, creative products are built from a synthesis of alternative approaches. For instance, cognitive-behavioral therapies combine behavioral therapies with cognitive ones. Ego-centered perfectionism can impair your ability to see past your own stale ideas!

To explore the effects of your ego-centered perfectionism, take some time to work on Exercise 9.2.

EXERCISE 9.2. How Has Your Ego-Centered Perfectionism Affected You?

In your journal, jot down, in detail, ways you think your ego-centered perfectionism has or may have negatively affected you as well as others. I know this is not easy, but awareness is a key factor in helping you to overcome this self-defeating habit!

So, are you ready to do something about your ego-centered perfectionism? Keeping in mind your reflections in Exercises 9.1 and 9.2, let's get started!

Step 1: Identify Your Irrational Thinking

The basic reasoning that drives your ego-centered perfectionism looks like this:

1. My point of view must always be right.

2. You disagree with my point of view.

3. Therefore, your view is wrong.

4. Therefore, I *can't* tolerate it.

In premise 1, you make the perfectionistic demand that reality conform to your subjective point of view—your beliefs, values, desires, preferences, interests, or tastes. When someone disagrees with you, you deduce that the person's view is wrong, so you *can't* tolerate it. And when you think you "can't" tolerate it, you won't!

Here's an example:

1. My point of view must always be right.

2. I like action thrillers better than your romantic comedies.

3. So, action thrillers are the best!

4. So, how can you expect me to sit through your movies?

Exercise 9.3 will help you take a look at the reasoning behind *your* ego-centered perfectionism.

EXERCISE 9.3. Identify Your Reasoning

Perform each activity and write down the results in your journal.

1. Think of a case in which a particular person disagreed with one of your strongly held views on a controversial subject, which disturbed you greatly. Maybe it was a political view or a view about a social issue such as abortion. Briefly describe your point of view—for example, "Abortion is always wrong."

2. Now write down your reasoning, using this reasoning template:

    1. My point of view must always be right.

    2. You disagree with my view that [*point of view*].

    3. Therefore, your view must be wrong.

    4. Therefore, I can't tolerate it.

Congratulations! Your completed template is the reasoning you used to upset yourself when someone disagrees with your point of view.

Step 2: Refute Your Irrational Premises

Let's begin by looking carefully at the "must" in premise 1.

Refute Your *Must*

In premise 1, you demand that reality conform to your subjective point of view. I get it; it can feel pretty good to be right about things. However, reality does not *have to* conform to what you want it to be. If it did, you'd never be wrong about anything—but that is plainly impossible. Anyway, would it really be so perfect if you were always right? You would never learn anything! And how boring it would be if everyone simply nodded in unison to your views.

Refute Your World-Revolves-Around-Me Thinking

Face it: the fact that others don't agree with you doesn't make them wrong. So you think that the political candidate you endorse is better than your coworker's choice, and you think your reasons are better than his? Well, it won't prove anything to call him a four-letter name because he refuses to agree with you.

Imagine that someone treated you this way. There you are, having your views trashed, or being personally attacked, by another self-proclaimed reality guru. Would you accept that? Clearly not! So what gives you the right to set *yourself* up as a reality guru? Why would your subjectivity be any more credible than anyone else's? Because it's *yours*? Anyone can make that same vacuous claim!

Refute Your *Can't*stipation

In premise 4, you declared that you *can't tolerate* the contrary view. But that doesn't follow logically from the fact that it is contrary. Of course, you can allow others to have their own contrary views, *if you want*. But *won't* is not the same as *can't*. "Can't" means it's *not possible* to tolerate differences of opinion. "Won't" means you choose not to. Unfortunately, when you *can't*stipate yourself by holding on to your "can't" and refusing to let it go, you don't relieve the cramps generated by your old stagnant ideas, unenlightened by alternative points of view!

Refute Your Pigeonholing of Reality

Perhaps the most glaring fallacy in ego-centered perfectionism is the assumption that reality can be neatly packaged into right or wrong, correct or incorrect, true or false, or real or fake. Your taste in music may be different from someone else's; you may have different political opinions; you may be interested in science, while another prefers the humanities; and you may value family above career. This does not mean that you are right and the other person is wrong. Reality comes in many colors and shades of gray, and it is illogical to attempt to reduce them to black or white.

Of course, some views are better defended than others. For example, a person may be mistaken about the facts or lack sufficient evidence. But your reasons are not better because they are *your* reasons. This is just the same old pigeonholing of reality into *I am right and you are wrong!*

Step 3: Identify Your Guiding Virtues

Instead of remaining trapped in this abyss of faulty thinking, here are three guiding virtues that can help you make peace with imperfection in a world where you do not always have to be right.

Empathy

Missing from the lives of ego-centered perfectionists is *reciprocal* sharing of subjective worlds. As discussed in Chapter Three, empathy involves the ability to connect cognitively, emotionally, and spiritually with others' subjective views. This ability builds mutual trust and willingness to speak candidly. Even if you agree to disagree, there can still be mutuality, respect, and authentic relating. In demanding unilateral agreement with your subjective world, you subvert the very possibility of such mutuality.

Tolerance

Tolerance is the antidote to saying "I can't" when you really mean "I won't." In this context, it means building the willpower to allow independent, diverse voices to have a fair hearing, even if you don't agree with them.

Objectivity

As you saw in Chapter Three, this guiding virtue cultivates openness to the nuances of reality and willingness to use rational argument instead of an irrational desire to be right. Just what the doctor ordered for overcoming ego-centered perfectionism!

Step 4: Gain Philosophical Wisdom from the Sages

To develop empathy, contemporary feminist thinker Blythe Clinchy says to play the "believing game": if I say something that seems absurd to you, instead of asking, "What are your arguments for such a silly view as that?" you ask, "What do you see?...Give me the vision in your head. You are having an experience I don't have; help me to have it" (Clinchy, 1998, 206). Instead of playing the doubting game, you make the effort to see what I'm seeing! Clinchy notes that this is just a *procedure* for knowing. It doesn't mean you will end up agreeing with what I'm saying. But, in *connecting* with me in this way, you get to see where I'm coming from and therefore to understand the way I see things from my subjective point of view. This in itself can help promote mutual respect: "Wow! I didn't realize that in your culture that's what people do!" and "I can see how you feel that way after going through such a harrowing experience."

Fritz Perls, existential thinker and founder of Gestalt psychotherapy, says that *to develop tolerance,* you need to use language that accepts your responsibility. Avoid language that shirks your responsibility, and replace it with language that accepts it (Perls, 2013). So rather than saying, "You pissed me off," say, "I pissed myself off," because it is you who does the getting pissed off! Likewise, don't say "I can't." This *can't*stipates you (keeps you from accepting responsibility). Instead, say, "I won't" or "I don't choose to…" The language you use is profoundly important for building tolerance for alternative perspectives, especially ones you may not like.

When you peel away these linguistic layers of self-oppression, you can better see how your own freedom is consistent with permitting others the freedom to cultivate their own subjective points of view. As Perls so eloquently expresses,

I do my thing and you do your thing.

I am not in this world to live up to your expectations

And you are not in this world to live up to mine.

You are you and I am I... (Counselling Connection, n.d.)

The eighteenth-century philosopher John Stuart Mill advises: *Let others choose for themselves*, since no one's perfect. Mill admonishes us not to interfere with others' life choices that do not concern us. Neither you nor anyone else has the whole truth and nothing but the truth. When you let others express their views too, even if some of these views turn out to be false, the whole truth has a better chance of eventually emerging than if you silence those views with which you disagree (Mill, 1859, ch. 3).

Buddha tells us to *have compassion for others* instead of being self-absorbed. Buddhism teaches tolerance as an essential virtue, since it can express love and compassion for those who do not agree with you (Ratnaghosa, n.d.). We are all in the same boat, trying to make sense of reality! By changing your attitude from self-interest to one of compassion for others, you can let go of your demand that others agree with you. And by letting go, you can experience great relief and inner peace.

To develop objectivity, says Francis Bacon, beware of the "idols of the mind" (false assumptions) to which human beings are prone. A sixteenth-century philosopher who laid the foundations of scientific inquiry, Bacon advises us to clear our minds of certain preconceptions that can destroy our ability to think objectively. These include the tendency to:

- Believe what you would prefer to believe ("I'm the best in the class at math")

- Ignore evidence inconsistent with your view (such as other students with higher exam scores)

- Make groundless distinctions and excuses to defend your own view ("The exams were unfair")

- Pigeonhole reality into perfectly ordered packages, even though reality is not so cut-and-dried ("Either you agree with me, or you must be wrong")

According to Bacon, all human beings have these tendencies to a greater or lesser degree. He calls them "idols of the mind" that we must guard against in order to be objective (Bacon, 2014). This calls for building a rational plan!

Step 5: Build a Rational Plan of Action

Of course, ego-centered perfectionists do not always respond in the same ways when others disagree with them. For instance, here are some common behavioral responses:

- Becoming obsessed with showing that those who disagree with them are wrong, bad people, or otherwise unworthy of respect

- Doggedly trying to get the disagreeing person to agree

- Making up "facts" (aka lies) to convince others that you are right

- Using emotionally charged language to personally attack, intimidate, or otherwise manipulate those who disagree with them ("What a wuss!" "Don't be a fool." "That's a crock.")

- Avoiding the contrary person, or acting unfriendly to the person

- Making threats

- Becoming physically aggressive

So what sort of behavioral responses do you have when others disagree with your point of view? Exercise 9.4 gives you an opportunity to explore these.

EXERCISE 9.4. What Are Your Behavioral Responses to Disagreement?

In your journal, list as many things as you can think of that you do when others disagree with your point of view.

What Would the Sages Tell You to Do Differently?

Our sages have time-tested advice for changing how you respond to disagreement:

CLINCHY

- Instead of attempting to manipulate, lie to, or call people nasty names, strive to see the world from their perspective.

MILL

- As a truth-seeker who genuinely cares about finding out the truth, give others a chance to express their points of view too so that the whole truth can come out.

- If you don't reach agreement, then agree to disagree!

- Everyone has a right to choose for themselves what to think and how to live, as long as they are not hurting anyone else. So stop trying to force others to think like you (Mill, 2011).

BUDDHA

- Let go of your ego-centered demand, and instead have compassion for others, even if they don't share your views. They too are trying to deal with reality in their own ways, just like you.

PERLS

- Instead of saying, "I *can't* tolerate others' views," say, "I won't" or "I don't choose to." Then take responsibility for your choice.

BACON

- Ask yourself what "idols of the mind" are impairing your objectivity, and then exercise your willpower to disregard them (Bacon, 2014).

With Exercise 9.5, see how these astute insights can guide you in constructing your own plan of action.

EXERCISE 9.5. Create Your Plan of Action

1. Identify your behavioral responses. In Exercise 9.4, you listed as many things as you could think of that you presently do when others disagree with you. Now revisit the sages and identify what each of these thinkers would tell you to do differently.

2. Create your plan of action. Based on these insights, make another list, of the things you would do differently. Be creative. *This new list will be your plan of action!*

Step 6: Put Your Plan of Action into Practice

It's showtime! This is where you implement the plan of action you developed in Exercise 9.5 to make progress toward your guiding virtues: empathy, tolerance, and objectivity. Chapter Fourteen will help you do this! As you work through that chapter, keep these three key ideas in mind:

- Your point of view is no more credible than that of anyone else simply because it's *yours*.

- You *can* tolerate alternative points of view if you choose to.

- If someone set himself up as a reality guru and tried to impose his points of view on you, how would you like it?

To implement your plan of action for making peace with others not always agreeing with you, proceed to Chapter Fourteen. Feel free to continue with the other type-specific chapters, but be sure you've first worked through Exercises 14.1 and 14.2.

CHAPTER 10

Treatment Perfectionism

Treatment perfectionists demand that other people never, or almost never, treat them badly, including in ways they think are

- Unfair or unjust ("They invited everyone but me")

- Unkind ("He wouldn't even give me a break, after all I've been through")

- Inconvenient ("I was planning to take a day off, and now he says I've got to work!")

- Unpleasant or painful ("It was so painful to hear his ugly opinion of me after I tried so hard to make the relationship work!")

- Discourteous, insensitive, inconsiderate, or rude ("He knew I lost my dad, and he didn't even send me a card!")

- Difficult or taxing ("Why does he always give so much homework?")

- Uncooperative ("Whenever I need him, he's not available!")

- Critical ("She told me my paper still needed a lot of work!")

- Unaffectionate ("He's so cold to me, even though we've known each other for so long")

- Unethical ("How could he lie to me like that?")

When treatment perfectionists believe they are or will be treated in such ways, their emotional responses may include:

- Anger

- Depression

- Sadness

- Irritability

- Anxiety

- Resentment

It's Understandable You're Upset

Undeniably, there are times when you truly have been treated badly (maybe even *very* badly), and it is understandable how you can be upset. You're only human, right? Nonetheless, you still need to give up your *mus*turbatory demand not to be treated badly; otherwise, you won't move forward in dealing with the reality that you were, indeed, treated like that.

Bad Treatments Are Not All Equally Bad

Of course, there are degrees of bad treatment, and it would be irrational to equate being raped or severely beaten with being inconvenienced or criticized.

But on the continuum between "Gee, that wasn't very nice of her" to, well, murder, most treatment perfectionism concerns treatment relatively low on the badness scale. With this in mind, let's take a closer look at some common types of treatment perfectionism.

Unwilling to Accept Criticism

This type of treatment perfectionist tends to wilt at the first sign of criticism, even if the criticism is intended to be constructive. She tends to perceive criticism as an assault on her personhood and may cry, become defensive, or avoid the source of the criticism. Consequently, she has difficulty holding down a job and advancing in the workplace. Such treatment perfectionists are also often achievement perfectionists (see Chapter Four) and therefore tend to become self-damning when it is suggested that their work product is subpar or that they adjust their work habits.

Prone to Moralizing

This type of treatment perfectionist tends to have an exceptionally high moral standard for others; consequently, it's easy for him to find fault with others. Examples of common "moral transgressions" are:

- "You show favoritism."

- "You're laughing at my expense!"

- "You're not really my friend."

- "I've never been so humiliated in all my life."

- "I feel like you're always taking advantage of me."

Unfortunately, the treatment perfectionist's response to the perceived affront is not usually proportional to the perceived transgression. The response may be unsociability, passive-aggressiveness, or strong resentment in the form of protestation ("I'm not going to work with you if this is how it's going to be!"). This poor person often alienates others, who grow tired of being accused of improprieties.

Ready to Counterattack

"You've messed with the wrong guy!" is the popular motto of this type of treatment perfectionist. "Just don't rub me the wrong way, and we'll get along just fine." But the rub is that it is hard *not* to rub this perfectionist the wrong way, and the consequence may be outright war—anything from physical confrontation to lawsuits! So much effort is wasted on fruitless hostility motivated by intense anger and a thirst for vengeance. And the results can be self-defeating! In one case, a disgruntled professor, angry about his teaching evaluation, declared war on the dean by attempting to organize faculty against him. This revolutionary ended up blacklisting himself among other administrators, and has since left in search of greener pastures. It is unlikely he will find any.

Easily Overwhelmed

This type of treatment perfectionist demands that others (such as employers, instructors, family, or friends) not overwork them or ask "too much" of them. I not infrequently encounter students who demand such "fair" treatment of their instructors. These poorly motivated students seek out classes where the instructor has earned a reputation for being "easy." In contrast, they indignantly perceive instructors who expect their students to work for their grades as "unfair" or "too hard." Because they tend to be discouraged when they must devote substantial time and effort to learning course materials, they often give up prematurely, fail the course, or attempt to withdraw. But the inherent and unavoidable challenges of life, especially without marketable skills, can be a great catalyst to constructive change, and I have found some showing up in my class years later, eager to work hard at learning. Better late than never, of course! Unfortunately, it has taken some of these students a decade or more to learn this lesson.

Loath to Be Inconvenienced

This type of treatment perfectionist demands that he not be inconvenienced or put out by others such as friends, family, children, significant others, and employers. "My time is money" is a common slogan; others are "I have better things to do with my life!" or "This is not a good time." They may experience anxiety, resentment, anger, or irritability when others:

- Distract them from their preferred goals or activities

- Ask them to do things at less-than-opportune times

- Assign them "busy work"

- Waste time with "small talk" or "boring" subjects

- Cause them even relatively minor injury or loss

Unfortunately, such individuals often lose the forest for the trees, and may not take the time to smell the proverbial roses along life's pathways—such as intimate moments with significant others, monumental occasions in the lives of children and grandchildren, helping a friend, and team or community efforts where everyone shares the grunt work to attain a collective good.

Exercise 10.1 will help you identify your treatment perfectionist type.

EXERCISE 10.1. What Kind of Treatment Perfectionist Are You?

Think about the following questions and write your responses in your journal.

1. Based on what you've read in this chapter so far, list some of the ways you think others mistreat you. Include the types of negative treatment you experience relatively frequently and have trouble dealing with. Do you have a difficult time dealing with criticism? What about being taken advantage of by others, excluded from social events, not being told the truth, and so on?

2. When others treat you in the ways you've listed, what feelings do you experience? Do you become irritable, angry, anxious, or depressed?

3. Can you identify with any of the examples of treatment perfectionism provided in this chapter? If so, which ones, and in what respect/s?

Keeping your responses to Exercise 10.1 in mind, let's get started on overcoming your treatment perfectionism!

Step 1: Identify Your Irrational Thinking

The basic reasoning that undergirds treatment perfectionism looks like this:

1. Others *must* never treat me badly.

2. You treated me badly (by doing such and such).

3. Therefore, it's *awful* how you treated me.

4. Therefore, I *can't stand* how you treated me.

Notice that my *mustur*batory demand for perfection together with my claim that you treated me in a particular bad way (for example, criticized, inconvenienced, or lied to me), leads to my conclusion that your treatment of me was awful. This leads to my *can'tsti*pation, when I tell myself I *can't stand* it.

So what does *your* treatment perfectionism reasoning look like? Exercise 10.2 can help you find out.

EXERCISE 10.2. Identify Your Reasoning

Follow these steps and write down the results in your journal.

1. In item 1 of Exercise 10.1, you listed the types of treatment that you experience relatively frequently and have a difficult time dealing with. Select one in which you believe you were mistreated *on a particular occasion*—one that was relatively minor (not a criminal offense), but nevertheless evoked strong feelings, such as intense anger, anxiety, resentment, or depression.

2. Describe the mistreatment you just selected, using as few words as possible: "Told me I was fat"; "Stood me up last night"; "Was dishonest about his true intentions."

3. Now, using this template, write down your reasoning, entering the mistreatment from question 2 where indicated:

    1. Others must never treat me badly.

2. You treated me badly when you [*mistreatment*].

3. Therefore, it's awful that you treated me like this.

4. Therefore, I can't stand how you treated me.

Congratulations! Your completed template is the reasoning you used to upset yourself when the person in question treated you in a way that you believed was bad.

Step 2: Refute Your Irrational Premises

Now, let's see which premises are irrational, and why.

Refute Your *Must*

Face it: others *will* treat you in ways you may, rightly or wrongly, think are bad. This is reality. So your *must* is hereby refuted by the facts of life. Unfortunately, this irrational *must* leads you to awfulize about your treatment when your demand for perfection is not met.

Refute Your Awfulizing

There is an important distinction between just *how badly* you were actually treated and whether it is *truly awful* that you were treated in this way.

Take this inference:

1. I was treated badly when you inconvenienced me.

2. Therefore, it's awful how you treated me.

When spelled out like this, the fallacy is glaringly obvious! In using the term "awful" (or synonyms like "horrible" or "terrible"), you are simply exaggerating just how bad it is. "Awful" means *extremely* bad; being inconvenienced is comparatively not so bad. Now, if the bad treatment in question was rape or a beating, we can understand how you would draw the conclusion that it was awful. But even for such awful treatment, you can still imagine something much worse—being boiled in oil on a slow simmer, for example. So, on the badness scale, being inconvenienced—along with most, if not all the other things treatment perfectionists routinely disturb themselves about—is not *so* bad!

Refute Your *Can't*stipation

Can't stand to be treated badly? Well, you literally can't stand up to a Mack truck coming at you at 100 miles per hour. You would be crushed by it! But you *can* ordinarily stand to be mocked, criticized, lied to, yelled at, stood up, ignored, laid off, cheated on, given the finger, worked too hard, given an unfair grade, sold a lemon, and countless other ways in which human beings mistreat each other.

Step 3: Identify Your Guiding Virtues

You should now see the irrationality of the premises you use to drive yourself bananas when you think others have treated you badly. Let's revisit three guiding virtues that can help you rise above this self-sabotaging reasoning and spare you needless stress.

Courage

In this context of perceived mistreatment by others, courage is the fortitude to:

- Place the relative badness of the mistreatment in perspective so as not to exaggerate just how bad it truly is

- Avoid, in turn, self-destructive behavioral and emotional responses

- Confront the challenge with measured reason

- Not be afraid to take reasonable steps to resolve it

"Well, that was a heartless thing to do, but it's not the worst thing anyone could have done to me. I'll just keep a cool head and deal with it."

Prudence

Prudence, in this context, means the habit of deliberating well about how to deal with the perceived wrongdoing to rectify the situation. This includes sometimes realizing that the one who can benefit from changing may be you, rather than the perceived offender. Here, prudence includes rational self-reflection and listening to the other side.

Patience

This virtue involves overcoming your *can'ts*tipation, which can prevent you from building and exercising courage and prudence. Proclaiming "I can't stand it" automatically disqualifies you from even trying to deal with your situation. Patience means having the *willpower* to listen to the other side, to not jump to premature and irrational conclusions, and to exercise forbearance in awaiting outcomes.

Step 4: Gain Philosophical Wisdom from the Sages

Granted that practicing these three virtues is a useful goal, how can you make progress in attaining them? Our illustrious sages have some powerful advice!

To develop courage, Epictetus tells us to compare what seems awful to things that are much worse: "Let death and exile, and all other things which appear terrible, be daily before your eyes, but death chiefly, and you will never entertain an abject thought..." (Epictetus, 1948, 21). This should put things into perspective when you are forcing a negative critic, an unfair professor, or even a cheating partner into the category that includes the infamous "Blind Torture Kill" mass murderer and horror film characters like Freddy Krueger.

Aristotle reminds us to *choose the mean between extremes*. He cautions that overreacting, like underreacting, is also a vice; that the rational approach avoids both these extremes; and that being courageous means:

- **Doing the right things:** Things in your control that can either undermine or fulfill your potential for happiness, by which he meant a life lived according to reason

- **From the right motive:** To remediate or improve your potential for happiness

- **In the right way:** In a way that supports your motive or goal

- **At the right time:** When taking action can produce the desired outcome

This is not exactly the picture painted by the treatment perfectionist who becomes angry, whiny, irritable, or depressed about a relatively minor mistreatment! Nor does it square with the person who acts out of blind revenge or to relieve anger or rage (Aristotle, 1941, bk. 2, ch. 6).

To develop prudence, Aristotle stresses action aimed at conflict resolution. Prudent people, he said, "can see what is good for themselves and what is good for men in general" (Aristotle, 1941, bk. 6, ch. 5). In other words, it's not only about your own happiness; it's also about the happiness of other human beings with whom you live, work, or socialize. So seeing both sides of the story goes with the territory: it means being open to a resolution or an understanding that is equitable in addressing others' concerns. It certainly eschews a blind, intemperate ejaculation of passion aimed at screwing someone you think screwed you, or manipulation of someone into feeling sorry for you. You don't have to make nice to someone who seriously hurt you, but you do need to exercise rational self-control.

To develop patience, Buddha says, we need compassion for others. Buddhism stresses the importance of patience as a virtue (Ratnaghosa, n.d.). Without it, given the imperfections of everyday life, you are vulnerable to a chaotic, stressed-out state of irritability, anger, and anguish. Things are not going your way? Well, without patience, you may curse the universe and go on a blind emotional rampage to improve your situation—only to make it worse.

Exercising patience requires positive emotion (Ratnaghosa, n.d.). Without compassion, you are likely to lose control and explode with anger: "That jerk just flipped me off! I'm gonna run him off the road!" That's no way to get through the hassles of everyday life.

Step 5: Build a Rational Plan of Action

As you read through these common ways treatment perfectionists may respond to perceived mistreatment, do any sound familiar?

- Becoming defensive ("Are you trying to say I'm a bad person?")

- Pouting or whining ("You don't really care about me")

- Having retributive ideation ("Just wait until you want something from me!"; "I'm gonna get you back!")

- Displaying aggression or threatening others ("Don't mess with me!"; "I'll show you!"; "Nobody talks to me like that!")

- Being passive-aggressive ("I don't really care, anyway"; "Whatever you say")

- Being confrontational ("Who do you think you're talking to?")

- Being antisocial ("Leave me alone!"; "Go away!")

- Becoming discouraged, trying to avoid further unpleasant encounters ("I'm not going to take this anymore")

So how do you act when you think others are mistreating you? Exercise 10.3 will help you address this important question.

EXERCISE 10.3. What Are Your Behavioral Responses?

In Exercise 10.1, you listed the ways in which you think others often mistreat you. When this happens, what are your behavioral responses? Do you become defensive, vindictive, or unfriendly? In your journal, list as many of your behavioral responses as you can think of.

What Would the Sages Tell You to Do Differently?

Our sages would offer these much more fruitful responses:

EPICTETUS

- The way you're being treated is only as bad as you think it is. Remember, it's not the events in your life that upset you, it's your interpretation of them, so compare it to something much, much worse, and then ask yourself if it's really as bad as you thought it was. This will help you see things differently and therefore *feel* differently.

ARISTOTLE

- Before you respond to those you think mistreat you, ask yourself three key questions:

  - Is your contemplated response likely to promote your happiness and not undermine it?

  - Is your motive to advance your happiness, not blind vengeance or some other potentially self-destructive motive?

  - Is this a timely response, neither too impetuous nor too late to matter?

  If you answered *no* to any of these, you had better change your response habits, because you are just making things worse for yourself. Aim for conflict resolution, which is likely to be in your best interest as well as theirs. These questions can get a dialogue going:

  - Why did you do that? Do you want to discuss it?

  - I would prefer not be treated like that. Can we talk about how to avoid this in the future?

  - Let's resolve this fairly. What do you think?

  - If you were in my position, how would you want to be treated?

Of course, not everyone is willing and able to engage in rational dialog, so use your discretion. Still, as Buddha astutely realized, having compassion for even the less rational among us can be helpful!

BUDDHA

- In having compassion for others, there is hope for peace of mind. Don't lose sight that we're all human, inhabit the same imperfect world, and encounter similar life challenges. "I suspect that poor fellow who just flipped me off is having a hard time controlling himself when he gets frustrated." Channel *your own* self-destructive energy into compassion for others, not contempt!

Now it's time to assemble your own plan of action. Exercise 10.4 can assist!

EXERCISE 10.4. Create Your Plan of Action

1. Identify your behavioral responses. In Exercise 10.3, you listed as many things as you could think of that you presently do when you believe others are treating you badly. Now, think about our sages' advice and what each might tell you to do differently. For example, suppose you become retributive and try to get back at those others. What would Buddha tell you to do differently?

2. Create your plan of action. Based on these insights, make another creative list of the things you would do differently. *This new list will be your plan of action!*

Step 6: Put Your Plan of Action into Practice

As you implement your plan of action, you'll be working toward becoming courageous in the face of perceived mistreatment by others, prudent in your responses to it, and patient about it. Here, too, you begin to *emotionally* accept the fact that others will sometimes treat you unfairly, inconsiderately, or otherwise not the way you would prefer. Keep these three key ideas in mind when you implement your plan of action:

- Being treated badly does not mean that the way you were treated was awful.

- You have the power to determine whether you were treated badly, and just how badly.

- You can ordinarily tolerate being treated badly.

To implement your plan of action for making peace with the imperfections in how others may treat you, proceed to Chapter Fourteen. Feel free to continue with the other type-specific chapters, but first work through Exercises 14.1 and 14.2.

CHAPTER 11

Existential Perfectionism

The world is a mixed bag of good and bad, right? Well, for existential perfectionists, this does not go down easily; for them, bad things *must* not ever (or almost ever) happen, or at least not seriously bad things. Existential perfectionists commonly experience high levels of persistent distress over:

- Bad things happening, or having happened, to them, their significant other, their children, or their friends

- The inevitability of death, aging, and disease, especially for them or those they love

- Social injustice such as racism, sexism, neglect of the poor, inadequate government support for veterans, discrimination against the LGBT community, and child abuse, among other forms of human rights violations

- Existential threats such as nuclear war, global warming, natural disasters, and famine

Existential perfectionists experience salient emotions such as:

- A sense of looming dread of something bad happening, even if good things are happening ("I just can't enjoy myself knowing there are bad things happening or going to happen")

- Depression or extreme sadness about the bad state of the world, oneself, or others ("This world really sucks")

- Constant angst about dying, aging, or getting sick ("How can I enjoy my life when I know I'm going to die someday?")

- A feeling of helplessness or futility ("What's the use of even trying when it all turns to dust, in the end?")

Now, let's take a closer look at these emotions and what they can portend for the lives of some people who demand perfection about existence.

"My Life Is Meaningless!"

One very perplexed soul came to me with the downcast view that her life was meaningless and lacked purpose. "What's the purpose of living when you're only going to die?" she demanded. "And what's the point when everybody I love is going to die too?" This poor woman saw her life as a sort of purgatory or holding cell until she faced her inevitable demise. Not that she was looking forward to an eternal hereafter—she was not sure that there was truly an afterlife. This doubt left her focusing on the futility of making plans when they were all going to terminate with her death and that of those she loves. Only when she gave up her demand that she and her loved ones remain permanent fixtures in the universe did she begin to live her life with a sense of purpose and meaning, even if it was not eternal.

"Humanity Is an Abomination"

This gentleman pointed to the evil deeds in the world as proof that human nature is, or tends to be, evil. "Look how many people blindly followed Hitler!" he proclaimed. "It could easily happen again, here in the U.S. too!" And he took as further evidence for his jaundiced view of humanity every instance of a bad actor, whether in his personal life, the lives of his friends and relatives, or as reported in the news. Whenever anyone did something kind, he waited for the other shoe to drop. People only *seemed* nice, until you found out what they were really like! He could draw only one conclusion: that humans were, by nature, selfish, untrustworthy creatures. So he felt uncomfortable around people, especially strangers, and he was very careful not to disclose too much about himself for fear it might be used against him. As a result, he alienated others and lived a relatively solitary existence.

"The World Is a Bad Place"

This fellow had been a deeply caring person, which led him to pursue emergency medicine (Wilson et al., 2017). However, after twenty years as an ER doc, he saw life in general through a bleak lens. He had treated children beaten into persistent vegetative states, mass shooting victims, teenage DOAs from drug overdoses; he had seen the ravages of end-stage terminal diseases and watched the steady decline of a beloved parent with dementia, as a spirited and kind personality descended into aggressive antisocial behavior. He had seen more deaths than had many of his colleagues who worked in private practice, an experience that included the never-easy task of breaking the bad news to the deceased's family. He came to see the whole world from his singular perspective. His relations with his family and friends became strained, and life for him seemed flat and dead.

Easy enough to understand how the poor doc might have come to this place, right? Sadly, he had entered the profession with the high-minded aspiration of saving lives on the front lines of medicine, but the negative parts of his practice took a toll, despite the many lives he actually did save. It was only after retirement and some good counsel that the doc began to open his eyes to the greater whole. He then realized his demand that the gruesome things he had experienced must not exist was blinding him to the good aspects of life—friends, family, children, grandchildren, even his dog!

"My Little Boy Is Sick Again!"

"How can he be sick again? He just got over the stomach virus!" the young mother said as she eyed the thermometer with astonishment. This devoted mom had become a regular at the ER with Jimmy, now six, who was prone to febrile seizures. Since Jimmy was an infant, she had lived on the edge of her seat, expecting the unthinkable. "I love him so much; if anything ever happened to him I'd…" There was simply no reprieve from her desperation. Crying *"No, not again!"* was howling at the moon. She felt helpless as the forces of evil again came down on her, taunting her with threats to the most precious being in the world. How horrible this was—like a never-ending nightmare, only it was real! The last time I spoke to this tortured soul, who refused to believe she could do anything about her suffering, she was still demanding that reality be other than it really was.

"Shit Doesn't *Just Happen!*"

This well-meaning middle-aged single father of three teenage daughters had had a run of bad luck. Six months earlier, his wife had divorced him and taken off for parts unknown with her lover. Then he'd been laid off from his job as a shoe salesman, and it was hard to find another job that paid enough to support a family of four. What was his explanation? There had to be some diabolical force in the universe whose goal was to destroy him! So he concluded that there was nothing he could do, and he was only going through the motions so he could tell himself he'd tried. Unfortunately, this fellow had a history of giving up. As a young man, he had dropped out of college after receiving an F in accounting and gone to work as a shoe salesman instead.

"This World Is No Place to Raise a Family!"

"How can I even seriously consider bringing children into this world with nuclear threats, terrorism, global warming, violent crime, and all the other craziness!" This morally conscious young man was convinced that the world was too bad a place for the proliferation of his species. His jaundiced view of the world impeded his strong desire to raise a family. It was not until he gave up his demand that the world not contain such existential threats that he could come to terms with his future plans. Last I saw him, he and his wife had welcomed a healthy baby girl, and he was enjoying fatherhood.

With these real-life examples to ponder, use Exercise 11.1 to explore your own existential perfectionism.

EXERCISE 11.1. What Existential Demands Are You Making?

Consider the following questions and write your responses in your journal.

1. Based on what you've read in this chapter so far, list the bad things you have difficulty dealing with—in your life, the lives of others, or the world at large. Do you have a hard time dealing with a string of bad luck or something unfortunate happening to you? What about getting sick, aging, or death and dying? What about existential threats, like the possibility of a nuclear war, or climate change and sea level rise?

2. What feelings are you experiencing about these things—do you feel helpless, lost, anxious, or depressed, or have a sense of dread?

3. Can you identify with any of the examples of existential perfectionism provided in this chapter? If so, which ones, and in what respect/s?

Based on your responses in Exercise 11.1, you should now have a clearer idea of your own existential demand/s and the feelings you are experiencing. Let's look at the reasoning that is generating these feelings.

Step 1: Identify Your Irrational Thinking

The basic reasoning driving existential perfectionism looks like this:

1. Bad things (of such and such sort) *must* not happen.

2. Therefore, if (such and such) bad things happen, then life (or the world) itself is bad.

3. Such and such bad things have happened, or will happen.

4. Therefore, life (or the world) itself is bad.

Premise 1 demands that bad things of a given kind not happen. For example, suppose you demand that you never grow old or die. So you conclude that, if this did happen, your whole life would be bad. It would be bad because this must never happen! Then you confirm the unthinkable—that you will grow old, at least if you don't die sooner! Accordingly, you conclude that your whole life is bad, even now, because you're going to grow old—or die first.

Now it's your turn to formulate your existential perfectionism reasoning. Exercise 11.2 can help!

EXERCISE 11.2. Identify Your Reasoning

Do the following and write down the results in your journal.

1. In item 1 of Exercise 11.1, you listed the bad things you struggle with. Now choose one with which you have particular difficulty coping, or the one you've dealt with most recently.

2. Describe this bad thing in as few words as possible: "Getting old," "Going blind," "Losing a child," "Getting fired," "The Holocaust," "Racism against black people," or you name it.

3. Using this, write down your reasoning in this template. For the global subject, enter what you are negatively rating—the world, your life, or life in general:

   1. [Bad thing] must not happen.

   2. Therefore, if this bad thing happens, [global subject] is bad.

   3. This bad thing [has happened/will happen].

   4. Therefore, [global subject] is bad.

Congratulations! Your completed template is the specific reasoning you use to upset yourself when demanding that the bad thing you described not happen.

Step 2: Refute Your Irrational Premises

Now that you've identified the reasoning that drives your existential perfectionism, let's debunk its irrational premises.

Refute Your *Must*

Shit happens! That's undeniable. To say that it must not happen *contradicts* your own admission that it has or will happen. I understand that you *prefer* that it not happen, but that's not the same as saying that it must not. Indeed, there's no contradiction in preferring that something not happen even if it has happened—or will happen.

Refute Your Existential Damnation

Premise 2 is absurd! Just because there's something bad about life does not mean that life itself is bad. Yep, you're going to grow old and die, or die and not grow old, but that doesn't make your whole life bad! What's true of the part is not necessarily true of the whole. Neither oxygen nor hydrogen alone is wet, but together they form water, which is wet. Baking soda is bitter, but that doesn't mean a cake made with it is also bitter. Your life and the world both have some bitter ingredients. But that doesn't make your life, or the world, bitter!

Step 3: Identify Your Guiding Virtues

Your existential perfectionistic reasoning would be laughable if it weren't so damn stressful and self-defeating. Fortunately, there's a way out of its clutches: to set your sights on higher ground—that is, the guiding virtues that can give you something bright and sunny to aim for.

Unconditional Life Acceptance

Trashing your life throws out the proverbial baby with the bathwater because it blinds you to the good things in life. Unconditional life acceptance means you are open to the good prospects as well as the bad.

Unconditional World Acceptance

Like your life, the world has its pros and cons. Living peacefully in the world means embracing the good even if it's not all perfect.

Scientific Thinking

Recall our shoe salesman. He thought there was a diabolical force afoot when things went wrong in his life. But a scientific outlook would not get hung up on such unverifiable beliefs. Being scientific means looking for explanations backed by facts. That doesn't mean you can't be religious as well as scientific; after all, whoever said religion and science must be enemies? But religion is supposed to lift you up, not drag you down into a dark cavern of despair.

Step 4: Gain Philosophical Wisdom from the Sages

So how can you aspire toward these three virtues, and be uplifted, not dragged down, by your irrational existential perfectionism demands? I know some more really cool sages with some constructive answers!

To be unconditionally life accepting, Friedrich Nietzsche says to embrace your fate. Nietzsche was a great proponent of affirming life here on earth: "I want to learn more and more to see as beautiful what is necessary in things; then I shall be one of those who make things beautiful. *Amor fati* [love of fate]: let that be my love henceforth!" (Nietzsche, 1974, 276).

Let me give you an idea of what Nietzsche means. I once heard a woman speak at a luncheon for human services workers. The woman, who worked in insurance sales, was led to the stage by a colleague. A few years earlier, she had been brutally attacked, blinded, and left for dead on the roadside, but she managed to survive. Disabled, she lost her job, and her husband abandoned her. This remarkable woman could have wallowed in self-pity and anger for the rest of her life. Instead, she remarried and became a champion for victims of domestic violence—the topic of her speech. Referring to her colleague who had led her to the stage, she jested, "I met my husband on a blind date!"

To be unconditionally world accepting, twentieth-century existentialist Martin Buber says to have an I-Thou relationship to the world. He draws on a distinction between I-It and I-Thou relationships (Buber, 2000). One can relate to the world as either an It or a Thou:

- In the I-It relationship, you focus on particular things in the world as objects, separate from you, to be used or manipulated in satisfying your desires. To complain that "those damn weeds have grown back again!" is to I-It your lawn.

- In contrast, in the I-Thou relationship, any distance between the world and you vanishes, and it's no longer about satisfying *your* interests or desires, because the world is to be revered in its own right.

To declare that "I am at one with nature, and nature with me" is to I-Thou your lawn, weeds and all. The same applies to other people. You can see them as Its to be managed or as Thous indissolubly bound up with you and all else in the universe!

John Hick challenges us to imagine what the world would be like without evil. This twentieth-century theologian is famous for his "soul building" argument that the evil in the world is necessary for developing good character (Hick, 2007). So if there weren't danger, there couldn't be courage; no disease, no great medical discoveries; no sorrow, no empathy; no needs, no beneficence; no bad deeds, no repentance or forgiveness; and so on and so on.

If you've ever focused on a single dark spot on the canvas of a great work of art, it may not stand out as beautiful. Seen in the context of the whole work of art, there may be an astounding beauty that could not exist were it not for that dark spot. This is not a plug for more evil in the world; however, keeping the overall gestalt in view without losing the proverbial forest for the trees can be an incredible antidote to a deep, self-destructive loss of hope.

To be scientific about the world, or life, William James recommends adopting a good-natured skepticism. This twentieth-century American pragmatist distinguished between the "absolute moralist" (read as "existential perfectionist") who demands that the world be perfectly good, and "he who in the main treats things with a degree of good-natured scepticism and radical levity" (James, 1912). Both adopt scientific explanations of the world, but only the latter gets verified by the facts. When shit happens, the good-natured skeptic simply adjusts his life to accommodate it: "I never said shit doesn't happen!" In contrast, when the absolute moralist's ideals clash with the world, he is not free to sacrifice his ideals to square with the facts, but instead finds himself "evermore thwarted and perplexed and bemuddled by the facts of the world."

Step 5: Build a Rational Plan of Action

The ways in which existential perfectionists deal with bad things that happen include:

- Giving up on life; not trying

- Crying uncontrollably

- Irritability

- Withdrawing from social contact

- Taking things out on others—for example, personally attacking or pointing fingers

- Procrastinating (putting off plans or tasks you intended to do)

- Taking alcohol or drugs to "feel better"

- Eating unhealthily—for example, bingeing on ice cream or candy

- Not eating

- Becoming obsessed—relentlessly going over and over what has happened with others, or in solitude

- Refusing to get out of bed, or excessively sleeping

So how do you currently deal with bad things? Complete Exercise 11.3 to answer this question.

EXERCISE 11.3. What Are Your Behavioral Responses?

Think about the difficult matter you chose in Exercise 11.2, item 1, and respond to these questions:

1. Have you exhibited any of the responses just listed? If so, which ones, and in what ways?

2. In your journal, list as many of your behavioral responses to this situation as you can think of.

What Would the Sages Tell You to Do Differently?

Here's what our sages would tell you.

NIETZSCHE

- It is self-defeating to wage war on difficult things. Instead, work with what is, and accept the challenge to bring something beautiful out of a difficult situation.

- Your attitude should be, "Well, if I had to live my life over again, I would choose to have the same fate I now have: *Amor fati!*"

- Don't get hung up on death because it interferes with living. Instead, affirm the inevitability of death as a reason to live while you're alive.

- Humor can sometimes help you capture the absurdities of human existence. For example, the woman who joked about meeting her husband on a blind date reframed the irony of how the tragedy in which she lost her vision had the good consequence of introducing her to her new husband.

BUBER

- Of course, you can't always I-Thou everything. You go to the store and, of practical necessity, treat the vendor as a supplier of your needs—in other words, as useful for a particular purpose, and thus as an It. But every now and then, stop to I-Thou the things and people you meet, both loved ones and strangers! Transcend your needs and desires to coalesce with the world, and the world with you. Feel this unity and connectedness in every-day interactions—walking outside, even in a crowded mall.

HICK

- Stop focusing on what is a virtual speck in the universe. It may seem big with your myopic vision, but look at the bigger picture!

- Ask yourself what virtues you can develop in overcoming your problems. Can you become more courageous? More charitable? More loving?

JAMES

- Be scientific; adopt a hypothesis of good-natured skepticism, so when something bad happens you are prepared, psychologically, to deal with it.

- Stop adding to the poop in the universe, or your life, by creating your own gloom and doom over it.

- Instead, have faith that you can deal with the bad things you face. When you tell yourself you're screwed, you will be prone to make that happen.

EXERCISE 11.4. Create Your Plan of Action

1. Identify your behavioral responses. In Exercise 11.3, you listed in your journal as many ways as you could think of in which you have responded to a bad situation. Now think about what our sages have advised, and what each might tell you to do differently. For example, what would Nietzsche tell you to do differently if you have become obsessed with your situation and constantly ruminate about it?

2. Create your plan of action. Based on these insights, make a creative list of the things you would do differently. *This new list will be your plan of action!*

Step 6: Put Your Plan of Action into Practice

Now it's time to put your plan of action to work! This will help you work toward your guiding virtues—unconditional life and world acceptance and scientific thinking. As you proceed, keep these three key ideas in mind:

*   If the world or your life *must* not contain bad things (or too many bad things), these things would not exist; but this is plainly false.

*   Just because the world or your life contains bad things does not mean that the world or your life is itself bad, because what's true of the part is not necessarily true of the whole.

*   You defeat your own purposes by tormenting yourself over the bad, since, as William James would admonish, you only make the world or your life worse.

To implement your plan of action for making peace with the existence of bad things in the world, proceed to Chapter Fourteen. Feel free to continue with the other type-specific chapters—but be sure you've first worked through Exercises 14.1 and 14.2.

CHAPTER 12

Neatness Perfectionism

Most of us like neatness in the world, right? When we have things orderly, organized, tidy, clean, in great condition, and free of any unsightly blemishes, they can be easier to navigate and look at. A messy desk can hide important records; a disorganized wardrobe can waste time in getting ready for work. A scratch on your car, a carpet stain, or a zit on your chin can be an eyesore. So what's wrong with wanting things to be neat and attractive? There's nothing wrong with wanting or preferring it. The problem arises when you *demand* it.

"Well, why should I have to look at that ugly stain?" "Why shouldn't I demand that the mess others make be cleaned up?" "Isn't it my right to live in an orderly environment, free from ugly clutter?"

Yes, you don't have to look at a certain stain, if you are in a position to get rid of or avoid it. What you cannot do is eradicate all the icky things and messiness to which you may be exposed. If you demand this, you are going to be a very unhappy camper. Why? Because the world is inherently imperfect; it has unavoidable stains and disorder built right into it: bloodstains; dog poop and pee accidents; mold growth from water leaks; backed-up toilets; the ravages of natural disasters; unsightly growths on the body as it ages; interruptions in orderly scheduling due to accidents, errors, even death; the mess created quite naturally by a small child; disruptions due to forgetfulness of others or yourself; and so on *ad nauseam*. You can definitely try to mitigate these things, but you can't escape the inherent untidiness of the real world.

People who are neatness perfectionists frequently suffer from:

- Intense anxiety about the possibility of someone or something making a mess or otherwise defacing their property

- Anger, even rage, when something of theirs is messed up by someone else, even a small child or pooch

- Guilty feelings about not cleaning something thoroughly enough

- Depression over not being able to maintain enough order in the household, or at work

Let's take a look at some common profiles of neatness perfectionists I have known.

Policing Neatness

This man patrolled his home looking for dirt anywhere he could find it. Friends and neighbors would be very impressed by how everything was in its place. "Like a model home," they'd comment. Not a single dining chair was out of place, because he demanded that his three children and his wife put their chairs back after eating. The floors were squeaky clean, and only stocking feet could touch them. All shoes had to be removed at the doorway, with no exceptions! If a departing family member had to go back into the house for a forgotten item, they had to take off their shoes, retrieve the item, and put the shoes on again. Furniture was gleaming and dustless. Every evening he would scout about looking for things out of place, or any trace of a stain, and he almost always seemed to find something wrong. Then he would issue orders in a panicky tone to "clean this mess up immediately!"

Masking the Signs of Aging

Since ancient times, the harmony, balance, and proportionality of the human body have been a dominant theme in works of art. On canvas or in three-dimensional space, artists have sought to capture the ideal form or essence of the human body. Unfortunately, more than a few flesh-and-blood human beings have attempted to turn their own bodies into perfect works of art through altering their natural endowments. This bodily form of neatness perfectionism has taken its toll on them.

One notable example: a forty-eight-year-old woman with a nineteen-year-old daughter was obsessed with her body. Taking great pride in sporting her enhanced cleavage, she was fond of sharing her daughter's clothing, and boasted about wearing the same size. With virtually every artificial filler and implant imaginable, she regularly checked herself carefully for any signs of aging. Demanding of herself that she remain forever young, this poor woman paid dearly with the anxiety of fighting a losing battle. The last time I saw her she seemed to have become a well-preserved caricature of herself.

A Girlfriend's Clutter

One former client of mine declared, "I like everything to be in perfect order." So when his girlfriend went shopping and deposited her shopping bags on his couches, he was distraught. He would immediately rearrange her items and find suitable places in his apartment for them so they no longer cluttered his living room. And while he did not say anything to his girlfriend about her "making a mess" in his abode, he sorely resented it and was considering breaking up with her because she was "inconsiderate" and a "slob." Fortunately, in working to overcome his perfectionistic demand for neatness, this client became less anxious and perturbed about his girlfriend's post-shopping habits.

The Routine

"I have a routine. After work I eat dinner, chill, and go to bed. Saturday is family day. Then on Sunday afternoon I watch a ball game." For this married man with one small child, this routine was not simply his preference; he demanded it, and was therefore unwilling to make alterations to it. For instance, when his wife suggested taking in a Sunday afternoon movie with hubby and child, the answer was, "No, I have a game!" "But can't you make an exception just this once?" "*No!*" This created a constant state of tension within the household. Behold consistency bought at the expense of family dysfunction!

Trying to Make Wood Perfect

I confess, I am a recovering neatness perfectionist of sorts, and I have had to work hard over the years to overcome it. For example, in my younger days I made wooden furniture, primarily for my children. I did it partly for the artistic side of working in wood, partly because I wanted to give my children something very personal as a monument of my love for them, and partly because I love wood and it was difficult for me to find affordable all-wood furniture. So making my own wooden furniture was a win-win!

Well, I would sand and sand, and still there were imperfections. The more I tried to get rid of imperfections, the more they would surface. Once I became so frustrated that I intentionally destroyed a piece of furniture I had been working on. "If it can't be perfect, it won't be at all!" was my irrational first premise. But peering down at the mess I'd made, I had a revelation that has directed much of my subsequent work—and my own recovery: "It's wood, after all. Wood is, by its nature, imperfect, and that is the beauty of wood!"

Yes, it was the *imperfections* in the wood that gave it character. Were it not for those imperfections, it could be just any piece of wood. But this distinct wood, with all its splendid imperfections, was part of what made my furniture unique and special! I have since generalized this idea to other material things in this world, and it has been very helpful to me in dealing with neatness perfectionism.

So now it's your turn to confess! In what ways do you demand neatness or orderliness? Reflect on this by doing Exercise 12.1.

EXERCISE 12.1. What Neatness Demands Are You Making?

Think about the following questions and write your responses in your journal.

1. Based on what you've read in this chapter so far, jot down the ways in which you demand order or neatness.

2. What feelings do you experience when your demands aren't satisfied? For example, do you feel guilty when you have left things out of order?

Do you feel anxious about other people making a mess? Are you mortified about having something unsightly on your body?

3. Can you identify with any of the examples of neatness perfectionism provided in this chapter? If so, which ones, and in what respect/s?

You should now have a handle on the ways in which you demand neatness or order and the emotions you experience when these demands are not met. So let's look at the thinking behind your neatness perfectionism and the feelings it generates.

Step 1: Identify Your Irrational Thinking

Typically, the reasoning that drives neatness perfectionism broadly looks like this:

1. Such-and-such must be perfectly neat/orderly.

2. It's not perfectly neat/orderly.

3. Therefore, it's (totally) bad.

4. Therefore, I can't stand it.

So, for example, in premise 1 you demand that your lawn be in perfect shape. But it's not in perfect shape—say, because you just noticed some weeds. So you deduce that your lawn is totally bad, and therefore you can't stand it.

Now complete Exercise 12.2 to formulate the reasoning behind *your* neatness perfectionism.

EXERCISE 12.2. Identify Your Reasoning

Do the following and write down the results in your journal.

1. In item 1 of Exercise 12.1, you noted the ways in which you demand neatness or order. From those, choose one that you tend to demand the most or are most concerned with.

2. Briefly describe it—for example, "My house"; "My complexion"; "My office"; "My floors"; "My daily routine."

3. Now you are ready to formulate your reasoning by filling in this reasoning template. For "neat" or "orderly," select the term most appropriate:

   1. [*Chosen item*] must be perfectly [*"neat" or "orderly"*].

   1. It's not perfectly [*"neat" or "orderly"*].

   2. Therefore, it's (totally) bad.

   3. Therefore, I can't stand it.

Congratulations! Your fleshed-out template is the reasoning you have used to upset yourself when your demand for neatness or orderliness is not satisfied!

Step 2: Refute Your Irrational Premises

You are now ready to expose the holes in your premises.

Refute Your *Must*

Premise 1 in your reasoning is absurd! Whatever *must* be perfectly neat or orderly would always *be* perfectly neat or orderly. However, *nothing* in this world is truly perfectly neat and orderly, much less always so. Look closely at even the most attractive face: there will be irregularities. Both sides will not be perfectly symmetrical; there will be skin irregularities; and so forth. Any order to this world also has its irregularities. Is your chair completely pushed in? To the naked eye, maybe, but not really, because objects have imperfect surfaces and therefore do not perfectly intersect.

Maybe you think there must be near-perfect order *all the time*. But this is plainly not so, since there is also plenty of disorder in this world. Even the most finely tuned processes and routines eventually break down, and any process or system involves a certain amount of entropy—that is, randomly distributed energy, or disorder. Face it: the world is not perfectly neat and orderly, and you are fighting a losing battle to demand otherwise!

Refute Your Damnation

So things don't *have* to be perfectly neat or orderly, and just because they aren't doesn't mean that they are totally bad. Of course, if your home is so messy that it is difficult to navigate, then it's time for some spring cleaning. But this is definitely not the problem of a neatness perfectionist like you who demands well beyond the degree of orderliness or neatness necessary for practical purposes. If you were to demand perfect neatness in order for something to be good, then nothing—yes, *nothing*—would ever be good, because, as you have just seen, nothing is perfectly neat or orderly. Further, what's true of the part of something is not necessarily true of the whole thing. Remember what I said about wood? Just because it has imperfections does not mean the wood itself is bad wood or the furniture made from this imperfect wood is bad furniture. To the contrary, the imperfections can give it character!

Step 3: Identify Your Guiding Virtues

So it is about time that you look beyond your obsessive demand for a tidy universe. You can do this by taking as your guiding virtues *unconditional world acceptance* and self-control in the exercise of *tolerance*. Let's consider each of these virtues in turn.

Unconditional World Acceptance

In this context, this means accepting the world as such, and any part of it (your body, your home, your furniture, your routine, your work environment), as inherently imperfect. It means feeling at home in this world despite its unavoidable flaws, blemishes, lack of order, and randomness.

Tolerance

To unconditionally accept this imperfect world implies the further virtue of self-control through tolerance for the imperfect nature of things. This means recognizing the difference between not wanting or choosing to accept the untidiness in things and *not being able* to accept it, and, in light of this distinction, exercising your willpower to choose to accept it.

Step 4: Gain Philosophical Wisdom from the Sages

To work toward unconditional world acceptance, Plato says to accept the perishable, changeable nature of the material world. Plato held that the material world we inhabit is an imperfect copy of the ideals of things that exist in heaven (Plato, 2009). So the chair you sit in is not the perfect chair, your house is not the perfect house, and you are not the perfect you. All these physical manifestations will eventually perish or die. Nothing in the material world lasts forever; its nature is to deteriorate and go out of existence. Perfection simply does not exist in this material world, so lest you expect heaven on earth, give up your demand! Look in a mirror. What do you see? Is the image you see perfect? Hell no! Well, your material body is also a sort of reflection or imperfect copy of the ideal you, which is nowhere to be found on earth.

Plato, among other ancient Greek thinkers, emphasized the functionality of things as an aspect of beauty. So, for example, even a wooden ladle that is worn can be beautiful because it works so well (Celkyte, n.d.).

St. Augustine, a Roman philosopher and theologian of the fourth century C.E., advises us to *rejoice in the beauty of the whole*. He further admonishes us not to get so obsessed with looking at the part of a pattern that "we cannot perceive the whole, in which these fragments that offend us are harmonized with the most accurate fitness and beauty" (Augustine, 1871, bk. 12, ch. 4). And he reminds us that the only truly perfect being is, by definition, God. So if you are telling yourself that you must be some sort of earthly god, give it up!

To work toward tolerating imperfection, Epictetus says, "Demand not that events should happen as you wish; but wish them to happen as they do happen, and you will go on well" (Epictetus, 1948, 8). When you say you can't stand certain flaws or lack of orderliness, think of Epictetus's directive: to accept the fact that things are just that way by their nature, and to push yourself to live accordingly. You cannot change the natural constitution of things (which is imperfect), so you are wasting your time in refusing to tolerate them (Epictetus, 1916, bk. 1, ch. 12).

Epictetus also tells us that "things in our control are opinion, pursuit, desire, aversion, and…our own actions," whereas "things not in our control are body, property, reputation, command, and…whatever are not our own actions" (Epictetus, 1948, 1). So while external things are outside your control, the way you think and react to them is in your control, which means you can always *choose to accept* these things.

Step 5: Build a Rational Plan of Action

The next step is to put these gems of wisdom to work to make progress toward your guiding virtues. Let's first look at what you are doing now, with an eye toward what you could do differently, based on the wisdom of the sages.

Here are some common behavioral responses that neatness perfectionists often engage in:

- Giving up on things (projects, plans, and so on) that aren't perfect

- Blaming others for their failure to be perfectly neat or orderly

- Becoming obsessed with getting rid of some minor imperfection (nick, dent, blemish, inconsistency)

- Procrastinating about doing something that won't be perfect

- Spending excessive amounts of time and money on trying to perfect their body

- Being hypervigilant in creating and/or enforcing policies or rules

- Not respecting boundaries (as in trying to fix some imperfection on someone else's person)

- Saying inappropriate or hurtful things about another's appearance (for example, focusing on the size of a person's nose, or a zit)

- Refusing to socialize because they're self-conscious about their appearance

- Being abusive physically and/or emotionally to others (for example, children or partner) when they are perceived as being not tidy or orderly enough

So how do *you* deal with situations in which you think things are not neat or orderly enough? Exercise 12.3 will help you sort this out.

EXERCISE 12.3. What Are Your Behavioral Responses?

Think of the neatness demand you identified in Exercise 12.2, item 1 and respond to the following questions:

1. Have you exhibited any of the common responses just listed? If so, which ones, and in what ways?

2. In your journal, list as many ways as you can think of in which you respond, behaviorally, when your demand is not satisfied.

What Would the Sages Tell You to Do Differently?

Now take a look at what our sages would tell you.

PLATO

*   Stop trying to make it perfect, because it's just an imperfect copy, anyway!

*   Consider whether something serves its practical function well, because this too can make it beautiful, even though not perfect. For example, if your house is livable, it needn't be perfect.

*   Don't give up on things because they're not perfect; if you did that, you'd give up on life!

*   Stop trying to perfect your body or anyone else's; bodies are physical things, which means they deteriorate and eventually die.

ST. AUGUSTINE

*   Instead of micro-analyzing things and stressing out over a blemish, stain, or other imperfection, look for the beauty in the whole of which it's a part.

- It's short-sighted to refuse to socialize or move forward with plans just because you perceive something wrong with your appearance. You are beautiful as a whole, and that's what really matters!

- If you have a disability, don't let it hold you back. Again, you are beautiful as a whole—and therefore you are a whole lot more than your disability. You have other capacities and aptitudes, too. Develop them!

- Seek to improve yourself, but remember that the only perfect being is God!

EPICTETUS

- Instead of saying "I can't" accept the untidiness of certain things, change your "can't" to "can," because aversions are in your power to control.

- Since you can also control your actions, push yourself to stop ruminating about shortcomings and move on with your life.

- Live according to nature: accept that, by their nature, bodies, houses, lawns, routines, desks, cars, and everything else in this material world are not perfect. Then stop procrastinating, giving up, avoiding others, or whatever else you are doing to deny nature.

Are you ready now to build your own plan of action? Exercise 12.4 will assist!

EXERCISE 12.4. Create Your Plan of Action

1. Identify your behavioral responses. In Exercise 12.3, you listed the ways you respond behaviorally when a particular neatness demand is not satisfied. Now, think about what our sages might tell you to do differently. For example, what would St. Augustine advise if your focus on the lack of perfect order in your office prevents you from focusing on your work?

2. Create your plan of action. Based on these insights, make a creative list of the things you would do differently. *This new list will be your plan of action!*

Step 6: Put Your Plan of Action into Practice

Now it's time to apply what you've learned in this chapter to work toward your guiding virtues—unconditional world acceptance and self-control through tolerance. You'll be putting the plan of action that you developed in Exercise 12.4 to work. As you begin this journey toward constructive change, please keep these three key ideas in mind:

- Perfect neatness and orderliness in the physical world is impossible, because all physical objects have irregularities and all processes include disorder.

- Since nothing in the physical world is perfectly neat and orderly, if you demand perfect neatness and orderliness for anything to be good, then nothing could ever be good.

- Just because a part of something lacks neatness or orderliness does not mean the whole lacks neatness or orderliness, because what's true of the part is not necessarily true of the whole.

To implement your plan of action for making peace with the lack of perfect neatness or order in the world, proceed to Chapter Fourteen. Feel free to continue with other type-specific chapters, but be sure you've worked through Exercises 14.1 and 14.2.

CHAPTER 13

Certainty Perfectionism

Certainty perfectionists demand certainty about what transpires in the material world—that is, the everyday world of physical events (events that occur in space and time). The primary emotional responses that such perfectionists experience in reacting to uncertainty are *intense anxiety and worry*.

The Definition of Certainty Perfectionism

The certainty perfectionist demands certainty *about the world*. This means that she demands perfect knowledge and assurance about the world, specifically about bad things happening. For the certainty perfectionist, having evidence that something bad *probably* won't happen is not good enough; she demands a 100 percent guarantee that it won't happen.

The Objects of Anxiety and Worry

Certainty perfectionists may experience anxiety and worry about:

- *Future* events, specifically with respect to the possibility of bad things happening

- *Past* events, specifically with respect to the possibility of bad things having already happened that they may not know about

- *Current* events, specifically with respect to the possibility of bad things going on right now that they may not know about

Future Possibilities as Objects of Anxiety and Worry

The future can be existentially challenging. We all exist in the present, which constantly slips into the past; what was once in the future turns into the now, and then into the past. So the future is something we never get to know with certainty before it happens. This not knowing can take its toll emotionally:

- Will my business venture prove successful?

- Will I get through these hard times?

- Will my child (whom I just rushed to the ER) be okay?

- Will I be laid off in the next round of budget cuts?

- Will I meet this fast-approaching project deadline?

In such cases, while it's human to experience anxiety and worry without reasonable assurance, certainty perfectionists *demand* certainty about what is inherently uncertain, leading to intense, debilitating anxiety.

Past Events as Objects of Anxiety and Worry

Not knowing whether or not something life-impacting *has happened* can, understandably, also be an object of anxiety and worry:

- "Was my loan approved, or not?"

- "Did I get accepted into that graduate program?"

- "Did I forget to lock the front door when I left this morning?"

- "Did her flight arrive safely?"

- "Were my lab results negative?"

In such cases, the certainty perfectionist "can't wait" to find out and demands 100 percent assurance, even if it's probable that all is well.

Current Events as Objects of Anxiety and Worry

Have you ever been in another room waiting for the results of a deliberation going on? If you were ever on trial awaiting a jury outcome, then you know the feeling. "If only I could be that fly on the wall!"

Did you ever have a severe pain in your chest? "Am I having a heart attack?" Indeed, in such cases of current events, the uncertainty of not knowing can be another abundant object of anxiety and worry. Unfortunately, the demand for certainty only adds self-defeating stress to the experience. So your chest muscles tighten, and the pain in your chest gets worse!

The Anxiety and Worry Experienced by Certainty Perfectionists

Some amount of anxiety and worry about past, present, and future events is normal. Not knowing whether you are having a heart attack, or your lab results indicate cancer, or your child will pull through can be daunting. Unfortunately, the certainty perfectionist's anxiety/worry alarm:

- Tends to sound even for less-serious things

- Tends to sound even for remote or slight possibilities of bad things happening

- Is ongoing and unremitting, so when one bout with anxiety or worry simmers down, there's likely another soon to follow

- Adversely affects cognitive abilities, such as rational thinking, memory, and perception

- Creates considerable stress for family and work relationships

- Can lead to depression

The following common examples of certainty perfectionism illustrate just how debilitating this form of perfectionism can be.

Taking Risks and Then Refusing to Accept Them

One twenty-nine-year-old male persistently questioned whether he had a fatal or life-threatening disease. When he was tired, he suspected leukemia, despite the obvious clue that he had not slept well the night before. Last I spoke to this fellow, he was in the midst of another health "crisis."

When Safe Is Not Safe Enough

This woman lived her life in a virtual prison. Afraid to take risks, she refused to drive, and relied on her husband to drive her places. She also refused to eat out in restaurants because they were not as sanitary as her own kitchen. On the couple's anniversary, her husband surprised her with two tickets to Hawaii. "This is so sweet, honey," she responded. "But you know how I feel about flying. Are those tickets refundable?"

Checking Up on Things to Make Sure

This professional woman drove herself crazy running back and forth from work to make sure everything was safe at home. Sometimes she would go home to make sure she'd unplugged the coffee maker or her curling iron, sometimes to make sure the home security alarm was on. (She was afraid to check it out online remotely because she thought she might mistakenly deactivate the system.) "I'm almost certain I pulled the plug out, but I'm not 100 percent sure." This ritual did not stop with constantly checking her home for safety concerns. It also manifested in her constant checking up on her children's welfare when they were at play; repeatedly asking her husband, who had a heart condition, whether he was okay; and checking to see how her mom was several times a day.

Afraid of Committing

This forty-five-year-old man had been going out with his girlfriend, Wendy, for ten years. They had gotten engaged five years before, but he never seemed to find the right time to tie the knot, despite Wendy's repeated prompting. "I really love Wendy," he declared, "but why can't we just stay the way we are? Getting married could ruin everything!" Unfortunately, Wendy decided not to wait any longer, met someone else, got married, and soon had a child. So what this gentleman seemed to fear the most came to fruition as a result of being afraid to take the plunge. This was a hard way to learn that living life is not a zero-sum game.

Keeping Mum for Fear of Blowing It

A former client of mine was a physics professor who could lecture on quantum mechanics to an audience of hundreds of colleagues, but he had a difficult time speaking one-on-one. Dating was especially challenging for him. "I just have nothing to say, so I sit there like a stooge." So what was he so afraid of? "I might say something thoughtless or odd." A vicious cycle: he would just sit there, speechless, because there was a chance that he might blow it if he spoke up. But that's exactly what he ended up doing anyway by keeping mum.

"I'm Not Sure I Can Breathe"

Panic attacks can be scary. Thinking and feeling like you are suffocating, helplessly gasping for breath, is understandably an experience to dread. This is how a twenty-two-year-old student described her experience whenever she went into a large store. So she avoided shopping centers and made special arrangements to have others do her shopping for her. She had been seeing a cognitive-behavioral therapist who gave her an assignment to visit a department store and to practice the cognitive-behavioral skills she was taught in therapy, but she was reluctant to complete the assignment. I asked what it would take for her to do what her therapist asked her to do, and she told me she needed to be sure that she wouldn't die.

I do not know if she ever completed the assignment her therapist had given her, but it is evident that her perfectionistic demand for certainty kept her from working through her problem.

Now, with Exercise 13.1, take some time to reflect on the ways in which you demand certainty.

EXERCISE 13.1. What Are You Demanding Certainty About?

Think about the following questions and write your responses in your journal.

1. Based on what you've read in this chapter so far, make a list of the things over which you demand certainty. Do you demand certainty about the future, the past, the present? If so, about what things in particular? Do you demand certainty that you're not getting sick, not hurting someone, or not failing, or certainty that these things won't happen? Do you demand certainty that you will not be treated badly by others? Are you afraid to take risks, even relatively small ones—for example, demanding certainty that you won't be wrong before speaking up about something important to you?

2. What feelings do you experience when you demand certainty about these things? Do you ever get depressed? Do you get physically ill—for example, with chest discomfort, palpitations, or nausea?

3. Can you identify with any of the examples of certainty perfectionism presented in this chapter? If so, which ones, and in what respect/s?

Keeping in mind the things over which you demand perfection, and the negative ways it may be affecting you emotionally and physically, let's see what we can do to help you feel and do better, using the six-step method.

Step 1: Identify Your Irrational Thinking

The general line of reasoning that drives certainty perfectionism looks like this:

1. I *must* always be certain that bad things, or specific bad things, do not happen.

2. Therefore, if I'm not certain, then I must worry and upset myself about these bad possibilities.

3. I'm not certain about a specific bad thing not happening.

4. Therefore, I must worry and upset myself about this bad possibility.

As you can see, in premise 1 you demand certainty about bad things not happening. From this premise you deduce that if you're not certain that they won't happen, you *must* worry and upset yourself about these bad possibilities. You think you have some kind of special duty to disturb yourself. Then you tell yourself you aren't certain about a particular thing (say, the possibility of your business venture failing). So you conclude that you have a duty to worry and upset yourself about this bad possibility.

With Exercise 13.2, you can personalize this line of reasoning to your own perceived need for certainty.

EXERCISE 13.2. Identify Your Reasoning

Do the following and write the results in your journal.

1. In item 1 of Exercise 13.1, you jotted down the things about which you demand certainty. Now choose one for which you most often, or very often, demand certainty.

2. Now very briefly describe what you just selected—for example, "my not having a heart attack"; "Jimmy not getting sick"; "my not failing the course"; "my relationship not ending badly like the others"; "my office mates not talking about me behind my back."

3. Using your description, fill in this template:

    1. I *must* always be certain that bad things, or certain bad things, do not happen.

    2. Therefore, if I'm not certain, then I must worry and upset myself about these bad possibilities.

    3. I'm not certain about [*what you demand certainty about*].

    4. Therefore, I must worry and upset myself about this bad possibility.

Congratulations! Your fleshed-out template is the reasoning you have used to upset yourself when you demand certainty.

Step 2: Refute Your Irrational Premises

Now look carefully at the "musts" in your premises for the purpose of debunking them.

Refute Your *Musts*

In the reasoning of Exercise 13.2, you have two *musts*, one deduced from the other. Look at the *must* in premise 1. If you truly had such certainty about the physical world, you would never be mistaken about bad things happening. But how many times have you been wrong? So you think you are certain that your plan will be successful, but still it ends up going awry. It has happened to you; it has happened to me. That's just the way the physical universe operates. You can have reasonable belief about it, but not certainty. So to demand that you have what you simply can't have is being utterly unrealistic!

Once you see that you simply can't have certainty about the physical world, you see that your second *must* in premise 2 makes no sense. What's the point in disturbing yourself that you don't have what you can't have? It's self-defeating. Presumably you are worrying because you don't want bad things to happen, but in making yourself so miserable, you actually *make something bad happen*, because intense worrying about what you can't have stresses you out without any overriding positive benefit.

"Oh, but won't worrying about bad things happening help me figure out how to stop them from happening?" No. Your worrying is excessive, well beyond what is needed to take reasonable precautions. To the contrary, as discussed in Chapter One, the anxiety generated through intense emotions such as excessive worrying actually tends to make it harder to think rationally about your situation.

Step 3: Identify Your Guiding Virtues

It's time, then, to set your sights on goals and aspirations that are more conducive to your health and happiness. Such goals, which can help you overcome your self-defeating habit of demanding certainty, include the following guiding virtues.

Foresightedness

In this context, being foresighted means making predictions about the future based on evidence, and accepting the inescapable fact that such evidence can yield, at most, probability—not certainty.

Scientific Thinking

Here, being scientific means you are prepared to learn from your mistakes in a process of trial and error and to accept that, in the end, all your beliefs about the physical world are subject to being corrected as you acquire new information. Thus, you view the act of knowing as a dynamic, ongoing process, not a stale set of unchangeable beliefs.

Decisiveness

Decisiveness in this context means having trust in your ability to make and act on decisions about the physical world, based on probability rather than certainty. You don't hold yourself back by telling yourself you can't act or decide unless you are *certain*.

Step 4: Gain Philosophical Wisdom from the Sages

If you were foresighted, scientific, and decisive, would you demand certainty? The answer is a resounding *no*. So how can you take steps toward attaining these virtues? The great sages of the ages have some helpful advice for you!

To attain foresightedness, the eighteenth-century British philosopher David Hume would admonish you not to confuse the evidence of the senses, which affords you probability only, and math, which yields certainty (Hume, 2011, secs. 20–21). Clearly, 2 plus 2 equals 4. Can you imagine it equals 5, or 6, or 10,000? Obviously not! It's certain and you can count on it. But what about whether you will do well on your exam, or get a nasty cold next month? Can you be certain about such matters of fact? No, says Hume, because you can imagine screwing up on the exam, or catching a doozy from a sneezing, runny-nosed friend. Note to self: the physical world, unlike math, is based on probability, not certainty!

To be a scientific thinker, Karl Popper, a famed twentieth-century philosopher of science, says to hold open the possibility that your beliefs about the physical world can be proven false in the future. Popper cautioned that no scientific belief is immune to being falsified (Popper, 1999). So looking for certainty in science is absurd. For example, if you are scientific about whether your business venture will succeed, you will keep an open mind about what the future may bring—big profits are possible, but so too are downturns in the economy. Certainty is out of the question!

To gain decisiveness, the existentialist psychologist Viktor Frankl says to embrace the uncertainty of life as a condition of finding meaning and purpose (Frankl, 2006). Demanding certainty blocks your potential for finding meaning and purpose in life, because meaning and purpose arise only when you are challenged, and the outcomes of challenges are, by their nature, uncertain (otherwise they would not be challenges!) (Frankl, n.d.). So in adversity, when the odds are stacked against you, you are particularly likely to find meaning and purpose, because the greater the uncertainty, the greater the challenge!

To gain decisiveness, William James says to have faith in your ability to achieve your goal. James cautions that demanding certainty can actually defeat your purposes. Let's say you are in a position from which the only escape is a dangerous leap; if you get hung up on the uncertainty of the outcome, you will likely lose your powers of concentration, be overcome with doubt, and plunge to your death. On the other hand, if you have *faith* that you can succeed, you will have a greater chance of succeeding (James, 1912).

Step 5: Build a Rational Plan of Action

Now it's time to build a plan of action. You can do this by looking first at the things you are presently doing as a result of your habit of demanding certainty and then at what our sages would tell you to do differently. So what are you presently doing, and what could you do differently based on your new insights?

Here are some common behavioral responses of certainty perfectionists:

- Procrastinating (putting off doing a challenging work assignment)

- Making decisions by indecision (not acting on an opportunity, so you miss out on it)

- Obsessively checking on things (like making sure the door is locked)

- Doing unnecessary things in order to "make sure" (undergoing unnecessary, costly medical tests)

- Avoiding making commitments (refusing to marry your fiancée)

- Refusing to take risks (staying at a dead-end job rather than pursuing potentially more rewarding employment)

- Not speaking up for fear of being proved wrong (remaining silent at a business meeting even though you have something useful to contribute)

- Defeating your purposes by worrying and making yourself anxious (worrying about the possibility that you won't do a good job and thus, through self-imposed stress, fulfill your own prophesy)

Now it's your turn to describe *your* behavioral responses. Exercise 13.3 can help with this task.

EXERCISE 13.3. What Are Your Behavioral Responses?

In Exercise 13.2, item 1, you chose something about which you most often, or often, demand certainty. Now respond to these questions regarding this demand.

1. Have you exhibited any of the common behavioral responses just listed? If so, which ones, and in what ways?

2. In your journal, make a comprehensive list of your behavioral responses when you demand certainty.

What Would the Sages Tell You to Do Differently?

By now you know that your habit of demanding certainty is self-defeating. Our sages' advice can help you attain your guiding virtues to overcome this habit.

HUME

- Accept that knowledge of the physical world yields only probability. ("I know I can't be certain the clear day that's forecast will happen, but that won't stop me from planning a day at the beach!")

- Proportion your degree of belief to the available evidence. ("That blood test is 99 percent accurate, which is good enough for me!")

- Be bold and decide or act, even without certainty, because if you wait for certainty, you will *never* decide or act. ("My market data shows the business has a reasonable chance of turning a profit, so I will run with it.")

POPPER

- Always be open to the possibility that even the most settled beliefs about the physical world could be disproven by future evidence. That way, you can revise your beliefs as new evidence becomes available. ("I used to think that my panic attacks could only be treated with the medication prescribed by my psychiatrist. Now I read there's evidence that cognitive-behavioral therapy can work too. I'll find a CBT therapist to help me work through my attacks.")

- You learn by trial and error, so be prepared to make mistakes. ("If I always had to be certain, how could I ever learn anything new?")

FRANKL

- Find meaning and purpose in your life by seeking out new challenges. ("When I announced I was going to be a philosophy major, everyone asked me what I was going to do with a degree in philosophy. Now I'm having the time of my life teaching young minds to think philosophically!")

- Life is inherently risky. Embrace uncertainty by taking risks. ("I never would have succeeded had I been too afraid to try!")

JAMES

- When you decide to do something, have faith that you will succeed. ("I know these are hard times, but we're going to get through them just fine!")

In light of the wisdom of our sages, what will you do differently? Exercise 13.4 can help you answer this question.

EXERCISE 13.4. Create Your Plan of Action

1. **Identify your behavioral responses.** In Exercise 13.2, you selected something about which you most often or very often demand certainty. Then in Exercise 13.3, you listed your behavioral responses when you demand certainty. Now, think about what our sages have advised and what each might tell you to do differently. For example, if you find your life boring but are afraid to take any risks to change it, what would Frankl tell you to do differently?

2. **Create your plan of action.** Based on these insights, make another list of the things you would do differently. Be creative. *This new list will be your plan of action!*

Step 6: Put Your Plan of Action into Practice

Are you ready to implement the plan of action you created in Exercise 13.4? This plan can help you overcome your habit of demanding certainty as you take steps toward attaining your guiding virtues—foresightedness, scientific thinking, and decisiveness. As you proceed, keep the following three key ideas in mind:

- It is not even possible to have certainty about the physical world (the world that exists in time and space), so to demand this is not rational.

- Life would be boring without uncertainty, risks, or chances.

- You don't need to be certain to have faith!

Congratulations on working through this chapter—and any other chapters you have followed through with. In Chapter Fourteen, you will begin putting your action plan to work.

CHAPTER 14

Putting Your Action Plan to Work

This chapter will help you implement the sixth and final step of our process for overcoming the ten types of perfectionism addressed in this book: putting into practice your plan of action! You have completed the five previous steps of this process in working to overcome a particular type—or types—of perfectionism. This includes having carefully worked through all of the exercises and using your journal to record your responses. If you are not at this point, then please be sure to do so before undertaking this chapter.

Let's get started with Exercise 14.1!

EXERCISE 14.1. Start Building Your New Skills!

1. At your earliest opportunity, start implementing the plan of action that you created in a previous chapter by doing as many of the things on your plan as possible.

   Be prepared to feel disinclined. You'll need to exercise your *willpower muscle* to start living in new and unfamiliar ways. You have been in a habit of demanding perfection and behaving in the self-defeating ways dictated by your demand. So the goal is to replace your perfectionistic disposition with a new, constructive one that is:

   • Based on the wisdom of the sages

   • Promotes your guiding virtues.

   The more you work at it, the easier it will become. So flex your willpower muscle! You can do it!

2. In making these behavioral changes, keep in mind the three key ideas introduced in step 6. Recite these ideas quietly to yourself before, during, and after you change your behavior.

3. After you implement anything on your behavioral plan, congratulate yourself and, at your first opportunity, celebrate by treating yourself to something you enjoy. This is important! Don't skimp; you deserve to be rewarded. In fact, for the process to work, suitable rewards are essential!

Now you are ready for some self-reflection with Exercise 14.2.

EXERCISE 14.2. Reflect on Your Experience

As you reflect on the following questions, jot down your thoughts in your journal so you can look back on your responses when contemplating and making further changes:

*   *What items in your action plan did you implement?*

*   *How did you feel when you were making these changes?*

*   *How do you feel now about having made these changes?*

*   *Would you add anything to your plan of action? If so, what?*

*   *What did you learn from implementing your plan of action?*

Moving Forward!

Please continue to work cognitively, behaviorally, and emotionally on your perfectionism by repeating Exercises 14.1 and 14.2. Remember, the key to freeing yourself from your self-destructive perfectionist habit lies in practice.

Keep in mind that each type-specific chapter in the book concluded by inviting you to Chapter Fourteen. So each time you work through a different type of perfectionism to which you are prone (as indicated by the Demanding Perfection Self-Check Inventory you took in Chapter Two), you should pursue your action plan for that type, and then you can explore other types too! Once you have worked through a particular type of perfectionism using the six-step method, you have a working understanding of the method. This skill set can help ease your task of tackling other types of perfectionism.

Last but not least, as discussed in Chapter One, the goal is recovery, not cure! As a recovering perfectionist, you will be subject to backsliding, so it is important to continue to work through the exercises in the chapters on your types of perfectionism. When you tell yourself, "I'm cured, I don't need to work at it anymore," that's when you are the most vulnerable to backsliding. Better to say, "I am doing well in recovering from my perfectionism. This doesn't mean I'm cured; I still need to keep working at it."

The reward for your dedication is that you can take a truckload of stress off yourself and others with whom you live, work, and socialize, and thus free yourself to excel at your meaningful life pursuits as you work toward your guiding virtues. I am confident that you have already begun to experience substantial stress relief as you make progress toward your guiding virtues. But, remember, *you will never be perfect*—never perfectly self- and other-respecting, never perfectly authentic, never perfectly prudent. *No one ever will be.* But you can continue to do better and better—and *that* is the goal.

So keep this book and your journal handy, and keep up the good work!

—Elliot D. Cohen, PhD

References

Foreword

David, D., Cotet, C., Matu, S., Mogoase, C., & Stefan, S. (2018). 50 years of rational emotive and cognitive behavioral therapy: A systematic review and meta analysis. *Journal of Clinical Psychology*, 74(3): 304–318.

Kazantzis, N., Luong, H. K., Usatoff, A. S., Impala, T., Yew, R. Y., & Hofmann, S. G. (2018). The processes of cognitive behavioral therapy: A review of meta-analyses. *Cognitive Therapy and Research*, 42(4): 349–357.

Lowndes, T. A., Egan, S. J., & McEvoy, P. M. (2018). Efficacy of brief guided self-help cognitive behavioral treatment for perfectionism in reducing perinatal depression and anxiety: A randomized controlled trial. *Cognitive Behaviour Therapy*, doi:10. 1080/16506073.1490810.

Introduction

Cohen, E. D. (1995). *Caution: Faulty thinking can be harmful to your happiness.* Ft. Pierce, FL: Trace-Wilco.

Cohen, E. D. (2007). *The new rational therapy: Thinking your way to serenity, success, and profound happiness.* Lanham, MD: Rowman & Littlefield.

Cohen, E. D. (2017). *Logic-based therapy and everyday emotions: A case-based approach.* Lanham, MD: Lexington Books.

Chapter 1

Cohen, E. D. (2003). *What would Aristotle do? Self-control through the power of reason.* Amherst, NY: Prometheus Books.

James, W. (1955). Some metaphysical problems pragmatically considered. In R. B. Perry (Ed.), *William James: Pragmatism.* New York: Meridian Books.

Chapter 2

Cohen, E. D. (2012). Is perfectionism a mental disorder? *International Journal of Applied Philosophy*, 26(2): 245–252.

Flett, G. L., Greene, A., & Hewitt, P. L. (2004). Dimensions of perfectionism and anxiety sensitivity. *Journal of Rational-Emotive and Cognitive-Behavior Therapy*, 22(1): 37–55.

Hewitt, P. L., & Flett, G. L. (1993). Dimensions of perfectionism, daily stress, and depression: A test of the specific vulnerability hypothesis. *Journal of Abnormal Psychology*, 102(1): 58–65.

Chapter 3

Aristotle. (1941). *Nichomachean ethics*. Trans. W. D. Ross. In R. McKeon (Ed.), *The basic works of Aristotle*. New York: Random House, 927–1112. Retrieved from https://ebooks.adelaide.edu.au/a/aristotle/nicomachean/book6.html

Cohen, E. D. (2007). *The new rational therapy: Thinking your way to serenity, success, and profound happiness*. Lanham, MD: Rowman & Littlefield.

Cohen, E. D. (2017). *Logic-based therapy and everyday emotions: A case-based approach*. Lanham, MD: Lexington Books.

Ellis, A. (2001). *Feeling better, getting better, staying better: Profound self-help therapy*. Santa Clarita, CA: Impact Publishing.

Epictetus. (1948). *Enchiridion*. Trans. T. W. Higginson. New York: The Liberal Arts Press. Retrieved from http://www.gutenberg.org/files/45109/45109.txt

Sartre, J. P. (1989). Existentialism is a humanism. In W. Kaufman (Ed.), *Existentialism from Dostoyevsky to Sartre*. New York: Meridian Publishing Company. Retrieved from https://www.marxists.org/reference/archive/sartre/works/exist/sartre.htm

Chapter 4

Aristotle. (1941). *Nichomachean ethics*. Trans. W. D. Ross. In R. McKeon (Ed.), *The basic works of Aristotle*. New York: Random House, 927–1112. Retrieved from https://ebooks.adelaide.edu.au/a/aristotle/nicomachean/book6.html

Cohen, E. D. (2007). *The new rational therapy: Thinking your way to serenity, success, and profound happiness*. Lanham, MD: Rowman & Littlefield.

Kant, I. (1964). *Groundwork of the metaphysics of morals*. Trans. H. J. Paton. New York: Harper & Row.

Kaufman, S. B. (2009). *The psychology of creative writing*. New York: Cambridge University Press.

Muoio, D. (2015, August). Dangerous dualities: Perfectionism and low self-esteem. Retrieved from http://blog.archprofile.com/archinsights/perfectionism-and-low-self-esteem

Sartre, J. P. (1989). Existentialism is a humanism. In W. Kaufman (Ed.), *Existentialism from Dostoyevsky to Sartre*. New York: Meridian Publishing Company. Retrieved from https://www.marxists.org/reference/archive/sartre/works/exist/sartre.htm

Chapter 5

Aristotle. (1941). *Nichomachean ethics*. Trans. W. D. Ross. In R. McKeon (Ed.), *The basic works of Aristotle*. New York: Random House, 927–1112. Retrieved from https://ebooks.adelaide.edu.au/a/aristotle/nicomachean/book6.html

de Beauvoir, S. (2000). Women in love. In Elliot D. Cohen (Ed.), *Philosophers at work: Issues and practice of philosophy*. Orlando, FL: Harcourt.

Ellis, A., & Grieger, R. (1977). *RET: Handbook of rational-emotive therapy*. New York: Springer Publishing Co.

Nietzsche, F. (1954). *Beyond good and evil*. In Helen Zimmern (Trans.), *The philosophy of Nietzsche*. New York: Random House.

Chapter 6

Aristotle. (1941). *Nichomachean ethics*. Trans. W. D. Ross. In R. McKeon (Ed.), *The basic works of Aristotle*. New York: Random House, 927–1112. Retrieved from https://ebooks.adelaide.edu.au/a/aristotle/nicomachean/book6.html

Burns, R. (n.d.). To a mouse. Trans. M. R. Burch. Retrieved from http://www.thehypertexts.com/Robert%20Burns%20Translations%20Modern%20English.htm

Declaration of Independence. (1776). Retrieved from http://www.ushistory.org/declaration/document

Hines, N. (2018). Why on earth is the Catholic Church making Mother Teresa a saint? Retrieved on August 8, 2018, from https://allthatsinteresting.com/mother-teresa-saint

Internet Encyclopedia of Philosophy. (n.d.). "Immanuel Kant." Retrieved from https://www.iep.utm.edu/kantview

Sartre, J. P. (1989). Existentialism is a humanism. In W. Kaufman (Ed.), *Existentialism from Dostoyevsky to Sartre*. New York: Meridian Publishing Company. Retrieved from https://www.marxists.org/reference/archive/sartre/works/exist/sartre.htm

Wagner, J. N. (2015, Spring). The Albert Schweitzer hospital in Lambaréné, Gabon. *Hektoen International: A Journal of Medical Humanities*. Retrieved from http://hekint.org/2017/02/23/the-albert-schweitzer-hospital-in-lambarene-gabon

Chapter 7

Epictetus. (1948). *Enchiridion*. Trans. T. W. Higginson. New York: The Liberal Arts Press. Retrieved from http://www.gutenberg.org/files/45109/45109.txt

Kant, I. (1964). Groundwork of the metaphysics of morals. Trans. H. J. Paton. New York: Harper & Row.

Lincoln, A. (1854, October 16). Speech on the Kansas-Nebraska Act. Retrieved from http://www.vlib.us/amdocs/texts/kansas.html

Rogers, C. (2012). *On becoming a person: A therapist's view of psychotherapy.* New York: Houghton Mifflin Harcourt.

Chapter 8

Ellis, A. (2001). *Feeling better, getting better, staying better: Profound self-help therapy.* Santa Clarita, CA: Impact Publishing.

Epictetus. (1948). *Enchiridion.* Trans. T. W. Higginson. New York: The Liberal Arts Press. Retrieved from http://www.gutenberg.org/files/45109/45109.txt

Hanh, T. N. (2011). *Peace is every breath: A practice for our busy lives.* New York: Harper-Collins.

Hobbes, T. (1939). Leviathan. In E. A. Burtt (Ed.), *The English philosophers from Bacon to Mill.* New York: Random House.

Sartre, J. P. (1989). Existentialism is a humanism. In W. Kaufman (Ed.), *Existentialism from Dostoyevsky to Sartre.* New York: Meridian Publishing Company. Retrieved from https://www.marxists.org/reference/archive/sartre/works/exist/sartre.htm

Chapter 9

Aristotle. (1941). *Metaphysics.* Trans. W. D. Ross. In R. McKeon (Ed.), *The basic works of Aristotle.* New York: Random House, 927–1112. Retrieved from http://classics. mit.edu/Aristotle/metaphysics.html

Bacon, F. (2014). *Novum organum.* Retrieved from https://www.gutenberg.org/files/45988/45988-h/45988-h.htm

Clinchy, B. M. (1998). *Knowledge, difference, and power: Essays inspired by women's ways of knowing.* New York: Basic Books.

Cohen, E. D. (2015). "I want, therefore it must be": Treating fascistic inferences in logic-based therapy. *Journal of Humanities Therapy,* 6(1): 61–73.

Cohen, E. D. (2017). The epistemology of narcissistic personality disorder. *Psychology Today.* Retrieved from https://www.psychologytoday. com/us/blog/what-would-aristotle-do/201709/the-epistemology-narcissistic-personality-disorder

Counselling Connection. (n.d.). Gestalt therapy: Overview and key concepts. Retrieved from http://www.counsellingconnection. com/index. php/2007/10/16/gestalt-therapy

Goleman, D. (1997). *Emotional Intelligence.* New York: Random House.

Mill, J. S. (1859). *On liberty.* London: John W. Parker & Son. Retrieved from https://www.gutenberg.org/files/34901/34901-h/34901-h.htm

Perls, F. (2013). *Gestalt therapy verbatim.* Gouldsboro, ME: Gestalt Journal Press.

Ratnaghosa. (n.d.). The art of disagreement: Talk four of six on patience or kshanti. Six talks on the Perfection of Patience. Retrieved from http://ratnaghosa.fwbo.net/kshantifour.html

Chapter 10

Aristotle. (1941). *Nichomachean ethics*. Trans. W. D. Ross. In R. McKeon (Ed.), *The basic works of Aristotle*. New York: Random House, 927–1112. Retrieved from https://ebooks.adelaide.edu.au/a/aristotle/nicomachean/book6.html

Epictetus. (1948). *Enchiridion*. Trans. T. W. Higginson. New York: The Liberal Arts Press. Retrieved from http://www.gutenberg.org/files/45109/45109. txt

Ratnaghosa. (n.d.). Kneeling in the snow. Six talks on the Perfection of Patience. Retrieved from http://ratnaghosa.fwbo.net/kshantitwo.html

Chapter 11

Buber, M. (2000). I and thou. In E. D. Cohen (Ed.), *Philosophers at work: Issues and practice of philosophy*, 533–537. Fort Worth, TX: Harcourt.

Hick, J. (2007). *Evil and the god of love* (2nd. ed.). New York: Palgrave Macmillan.

James, W. (1912). The sentiment of rationality. In W. James, *The will to believe and other essays in popular philosophy*. New York: Longman, Green, & Co. Retrieved from http://www.gutenberg.org/ebooks/26659

Nietzsche, F. (1974). *The gay science*. Trans. W. Kaufmann. New York: Vintage.

Wilson, W., Raj, J. P., Narayan, G., Ghiya, M., Murty, S., & Joseph, B. (2017). Quantifying burnout among emergency medicine professionals. *Journal of Emergency Trauma Shock*, 10(4): 199–204.

Chapter 12

Augustine, A. (1871). *City of God*. Volume 1. New York: Charles Scribner & Sons. Retrieved from http://www.gutenberg.org/files/45304/45304-h/45304 -h.htm

Celkyte, A. (n.d.). Ancient aesthetics. In *Internet Encyclopedia of Philosophy*. Retrieved from www.iep. utm.edu/anc-aest

Epictetus. (1916). *Discourses*. Trans. P. E. Matheson. In *The discourses and manual, together with fragments of his writings*. Oxford: The Clarendon Press. Retrieved from http://www.sacred-texts. com/cla/dep/index.htm

Epictetus. (1948). *Enchiridion*. Trans. T. W. Higginson. New York: The Liberal Arts Press. Retrieved from http://www.gutenberg.org/files/45109/45109.txt

Plato. (1888). *The republic*. Trans. Benjamin Jowett. Oxford: The Clarendon Press. Retrieved from http://classics.mit.edu/Plato/republic.html

Chapter 13

Frankl, V. E. (n.d.). On challenges, dreams, and emotion. Victor Frankl Institute of Logotherapy in Israel. Retrieved from http://themeaningseeker.org/on -challenge-dreams-and-emotion

Frankl, V. E. (2006). *Man's search for meaning*. New York: Random House.

Hume, D. (2011). An enquiry concerning human understanding. Ed. L. A. Selby-Bigge. Retrieved from http://www.gutenberg.org/files/9662/9662-h /9662-h. htm#section4

James, W. (1912). The will to believe. In W. James, *The will to believe and other essays in popular philosophy*. New York: Longman, Green, & Co. Retrieved from http://www.gutenberg.org/ebooks/26659

Popper, K. (1999). *All life is problem solving*. London: Routledge.

Elliot D. Cohen, PhD, is professor and chair of the department of humanities at Indian River State College, adjunct professor of clinical ethics at the Florida State University College of Medicine, and director of the Logic-Based Therapy & Consultation Institute. Author of numerous books and articles, he is a principal founder of philosophical counseling in the United States, and inventor of logic-based therapy. He writes a blog for *Psychology Today*, and has been quoted in major media venues, including the *New York Times Magazine*.

Foreword writer **William J. Knaus EdD**, is a licensed psychologist with more than forty years of clinical experience working with people suffering from anger, anxiety, depression, and procrastination. He is author and coauthor of several books, including *The Cognitive Behavioral Workbook for Depression* and *The Cognitive Behavioral Workbook for Anxiety*.